THE SECOND WORLD
IN PHOTOGRAPHS

1939

THE SECOND WORLD WAR AT SEA
IN PHOTOGRAPHS

1939

PHIL CARRADICE

AMBERLEY

First published 2014

Amberley Publishing
The Hill, Stroud
Gloucestershire, GL5 4EP

www.amberley-books.com

British Library Cataloguing in Publication Data.
A catalogue record for this book is available from the British Library.

ISBN 978 1 4456 2235 4 (print)
ISBN 978 1 4456 2258 3 (ebook)

Typeset in 10pt on 12pt Sabon.
Typesetting and Origination by Amberley Publishing.
Printed in the UK.

Contents

Background

If anyone is looking for the origins or the seeds of the Second World War, they can be found in the humiliating treaties of Versailles and St Germain, which were signed in the spring and early summer of 1919. These were the peace agreements that brought to an end the first major conflict of the twentieth century, the First World War.

The treaties were debated and forged in the absence of Germany, something that should have alerted the German people to the way the victorious nations were thinking. Once decisions had been made, the German representatives of the defeated enemy were then summoned to the Hall of Mirrors at the Palace of Versailles and told what would happen. The message was simple: accept the terms or the war begins again – something Germany was neither emotionally nor practically willing to even contemplate.

By the terms of the treaties, Germany was labelled as the major instigator of the First World War. More than that, she was considered to be the major aggressor in the conflict, and the main harbinger of death for 10 million men. To anyone who attended the Peace Conference, or even to those who simply read the papers, it was clear that the mood of revenge was in the air. Not even the restraining hand of British Prime Minister David Lloyd George, limited as it was, could prevent the vindictiveness of French Premier Clemenceau – the man who once declared, 'I wish to be buried standing up, facing Germany' – from shining through.

War guilt was the predominant theme of the discussions. Despite her devastated economy and state of near bankruptcy, in the eyes of the delegates at Versailles, Germany had to be seen to pay for her actions.

As a consequence, valuable industrial land was taken from her, and either handed over to nations like France or fashioned into new countries that had little purpose other than to store up problems for the years ahead. Germany lost all her overseas colonies, while significant parts of the home country itself were occupied by foreign troops. She was also forced to pay crippling reparations to the victorious nations.

For the armed forces there was similar sweeping punishment. The army was reduced to just 100,000 men, the German air force ceased to exist and the High

Seas Fleet – the ships that had been the pride and joy of the eternally adolescent Kaiser Wilhelm – was taken into useless and rusting captivity in Scapa Flow. For the foreseeable future, the German Navy was to be limited to just six old battleships, six light cruisers, twelve destroyers and a number of smaller craft.

Significantly, Germany was to be allowed no submarines. Britain, only too conscious of how close the U-boat blockade of 1917–1918 had come to bringing the country to its knees, was taking no risks. In 1919, destroying the submarine arm of the German Navy – the Reichsmarine as it was known until 1935 – seemed an eminently sensible thing to do.

The punitive Treaty of Versailles was hugely counterproductive, and caused bitter resentment in Germany. As the Weimar Republic, created in the wake of the Kaiser's abdication, disintegrated into chaos and confusion, and as the economic hardships of the late 1920s bit into what little security the Germans had left, people turned in desperation to the extremes of the political right and left. The rabble-rousing Communists and Nazis at least promised some sort of salvation, albeit in different ways.

Riots, attempted coups and pitched battles on the streets symbolised Germany in the late 1920s and early 1930s, as people tried to make sense of the twilight world into which they had been tipped. The value of the Mark plummeted and people lost their life savings overnight. Starvation was a real prospect for many.

The troubles were not all down to the Treaty of Versailles, but that was a useful peg on which people could hang their disgruntlement. The treaty had not brought peace and contentment, only anarchy. Small wonder that bitterness was rife.

Adolf Hitler and his Nazi Party were ultimately successful in climbing to the top of a very precarious, not to say dangerous, heap. Despite the opposition of President Hindenberg, Hitler was appointed Chancellor at the end of January 1933. He had got there by promising dynamic leadership that would restore order and prosperity to the shattered country. Having come to power democratically, he immediately set about creating his dictatorship, secretly rearming Germany and equipping her to resume what he and his followers felt was her rightful position in the world.

Almost immediately, the size of the army was increased. The Allied powers did nothing. In 1935, Hitler announced the reforming of a German air force – again, France and Britain did nothing. That left only the navy.

With the number and strength of its ships still limited by the Treaty of Versailles, any building of warships in Germany needed to be surreptitious. However, the hidden hand of naval planners had already been at work long before Hitler came to power. In the early 1920s, a number of fast, modern freighters had been commissioned – banana boats as they were known – supposedly for the German mercantile marine but actually designed for military use as armed merchant cruisers at some stage in the future.

In 1922, the German Navy obtained an interest in a Dutch design company and their leading German submarine designers were soon toiling away. They were supposedly designing vessels for foreign countries but they were also developing their skills and talents. More importantly, they were waiting for the moment when somebody back in Germany was prepared to throw off the shackles of the Treaty of Versailles and order U-boats to be built once more.

The terms of the Treaty of Versailles allowed Germany to replace old and worn out ships as long as they were within a 10,000-ton limit. This resulted in the Deutschland Class of heavy cruiser. These brand-new ships were fast and well armed, and are sometimes known as pocket battleships. They pre-date Hitler's rise to power, the *Deutschland* herself being launched in May 1929. Once the Nazis assumed control, however, they automatically pushed at the boundaries of the various treaty limitations, with the result that the pocket battleships have always been considered part of the Nazi rebuilding programme.

From 1933 onwards Hitler developed brinkmanship to a fine art. Faced by appeasing nations, who seemed willing to do anything rather than start a new war, the obvious comparison is with the playground bully who always seems to know exactly how far he can go. The design and finish of Hitler's powerful pocket battleships is a classic example of the process.

The British rigidly adhered to the treaty limitations, not so Adolf Hitler. The *Admiral Graf Spee*, laid down in October 1932, was not completed until 1936, and although she was nominally under 10,000 tons her full load displacement was 16,280 tons, well over the Versailles limit. Her six 11-inch guns and a top speed of 28 knots made her more than a match for any British 'treaty cruiser' of the time. It is inconceivable that the British did not know what Germany was doing, but for some reason nobody seemed willing to challenge Hitler.

Even so, it was 1935 before Hitler felt confident enough to risk building a small U-boat arm for his navy, the Kriegsmarine as it was now known. Only days after the British–German Naval Treaty, which limited the size and strength of the respective British and German fleets – an agreement which Hitler, with the creation of massive warships like the *Bismarck* and *Tirpitz*, promptly ignored – the sleek grey shape of U1 slid easily into the waters of Kiel dockyard.

The 1935 Naval Treaty had limited Germany to a U-boat fleet of just 31,500 standard tonnes, small enough by anyone's reckoning. It was the start of a process, however, and in 1938, just twelve months before the war broke out, this figure was raised to 70,000 tonnes. It meant that on 1 September 1939, Germany had fifty-seven U-boats in service. Seven more were launched and equipped before the end of the year, and in 1940 over fifty new U-boats were added to the fleet.

Quite what the British naval strategists were thinking remains unclear. The presence of the High Seas Fleet had been a hollow enough threat during the First World War. Despite the drawn Battle of Jutland, the German Dreadnoughts could not hope to really challenge the might of the Royal Navy. The submarine threat, however, was a very different matter.

Many thousands of tons of shipping – British, Allied and neutral – had been sent to the bottom of the ocean during 1917 and 1918, destroying valuable supplies and provisions, and it had soon become clear that Germany's best chance of defeating Britain lay not in capital ships but in the tiny, cramped and dangerous hulls of her U-boat fleet. All the effort and energy of the German Navy during the final two years of the war was directed at the success of the U-boat campaign; and it nearly worked.

The establishment of a convoy system, new improved escort vessels and the development of effective ways of detecting submarines saved Britain in 1918. It was hard, unglamorous work but it was an essential victory for the Royal Navy.

Despite having been brought to within an inch of defeat by the U-boat attacks on its commerce in 1917 and early 1918, by allowing Germany to begin building a submarine fleet Britain was now in the process of letting the same thing to happen again. At a time when Hitler was sabre rattling around Europe and making his intentions perfectly obvious for all to see, it was a practice and policy that was verging on the criminal.

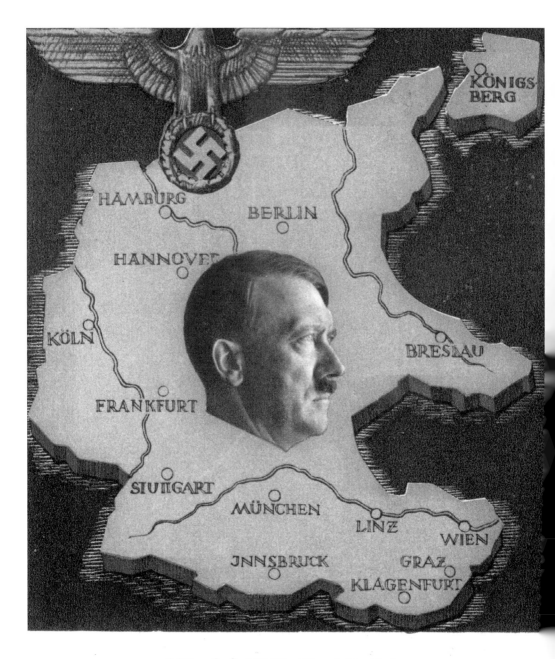

13·MÄRZ 1938
EIN VOLK EIN REICH
EIN FÜHRER

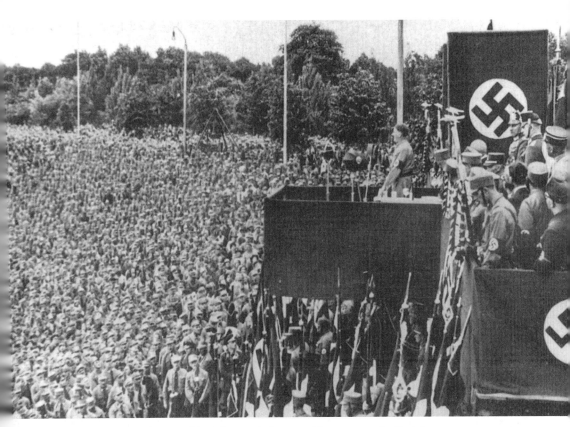

Hitler addresses his adoring public. Thousands hang on his every word, all of them eager to see Germany re-establish herself in a position of power in the world. The Kriegsmarine was to play an important role in that re-emergence, although, even then, Hitler had doubts about the ability of his giant surface craft to compete with the Royal Navy. Karl Dönitz and his U-boats might clearly be a much safer bet.

Opposite page: 'One people, one country, one leader', reads this Nazi Party propaganda postcard from 1938, when Germany had begun to rearm and Hitler had already annexed Austria. By now, he was also preparing to make his other territorial demands in Europe. The German Navy, the Kriegsmarine, had already begun building an enormous U-boat fleet while pocket battleships like the *Admiral Graf Spee* and *Deutschland* were astounding the world by their grace, beauty and raw power.

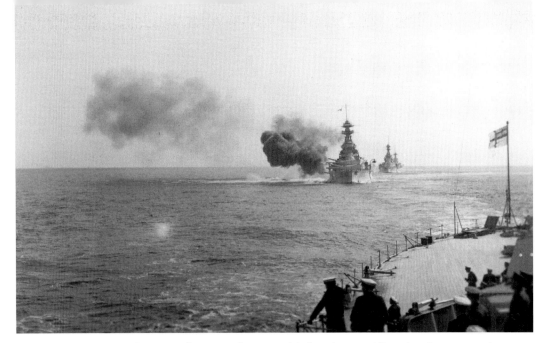

In 1939, the Royal Navy still possessed a powerful fleet, but, rapidly aging, it was one that would have been more at home at Jutland than facing the guns of the modern German Navy. The battle fleet may have been substantial and, as Hitler instinctively felt, no foreign power would have relished going up against the guns of ships like the *Barham*, *Warspite*, *Nelson* and *Rodney*. However, anti-submarine vessels were almost non-existent. It was a major weakness that would be cruelly exploited when war broke out on 3 September.

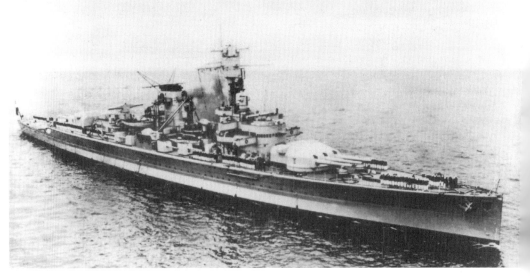

The *Deutschland*, launched in 1929, was the first of Germany's new big-gun ships. Hitler embraced her – and her sister ship *Graf Spee* – but, contrary to popular belief, he did not actually commission either of the two pocket battleships, which were either in service or had already been laid down when he came to power.

The War at Sea, 1939

When war broke out on 3 September 1939, the Royal Navy had just 150 destroyers in commission and no aircraft that could be employed on any form of anti-submarine work. In complete contrast, in November 1918 the Navy had been able to boast 257 escort vessels and over 500 aircraft and airships – along with another 500 smaller craft that could be deployed when needed.

Unfortunately, the success of the convoy system, combined with the development of ASDIC (the Allied Submarine Detection Investigation Committee) in 1918, had led to misplaced optimism at the Admiralty. During the 1920s and 1930s, the anti-submarine and escort arm of the Navy had been run almost out of existence. The day of the submarine, many people felt, was over. It took only a few days of war for that opinion to be changed.

Britain's battle fleet was still a significant threat to any naval opponent, but by 1939 there was a preponderance of old ships, vessels that would have been quite at home in 1914–18 but that were now almost out of date. A programme of building more capital ships was set in motion in the final years of the 1930s, as war loomed ever closer, but it would take time for these vessels to come into service.

In the eyes of many, it was a case of too little, too late. Preparations for war, however, were also going on in other quarters.

On 12 April 1939, the Womens Royal Naval Service was reformed. Originally established in 1917, its purpose was to place women into positions where they could take on the jobs previously given to men who could and should have been in service afloat.

The WRNS were disbanded in 1919, after the end of the First World War, when it was felt that there was no longer any need to free up men for the fleet. However, in early 1939, with war clearly coming again, it was decided to recreate the service. By September there were 1,000 WRNS – cooks, drivers, writers and so on – serving in the Navy, a figure that had grown to 74,000 by 1944. In the post-war years, it was quickly decided that the women workers were indispensable, and they became an integral part of the Navy.

Britain depended on the Royal Navy to protect its shores, although it arguably depended on its merchant fleet even more. Without the cargo vessels and tramp steamers, without the oil tankers and passenger ships, trade would simply dry up, and the population of the country would starve.

In 1939 there were almost 4,000 cargo ships, coasters and oil tankers registered in Britain, over 21 million tons of shipping. On any given day, well over 2,000 British ships – along with a host of foreign vessels – were at sea, bound for or heading away from British ports. These were the vessels that brought in the vital food supplies and raw materials that kept the country running.

Karl Dönitz, head of the German submarine arm, was clear that the most effective way of defeating Britain was to attack and destroy her merchant marine. At first, the Kriegsmarine might have been slow to follow his advice or thinking, but as the war ground relentlessly on, the U-boat and convoy battles would become the most fearsome aspect of the whole conflict.

September

On 1 September the old German battleship *Schleswig Holstein*, then operating as a training ship for new recruits, set the Second World War in motion when she opened fire on the Westerplatte, a long neck of land jutting out into the Vistula estuary that was the base for a Polish military garrison. German land forces, backed by the Luftwaffe, immediately stormed into Poland. The leaders of Britain and France, finally realising that Adolf Hitler was not the man to compromise or do business with, were stung into action, and they declared war on Germany a few days later.

In many respects it was an empty gesture, as neither Britain nor France could do more than complain or pontificate as Poland was overrun. The war in the west, for a long while at least, did not happen. The men of the BEF were sent to France, kicking their heels in Flanders and along the Belgian border while the French army sat confidently in the giant bunkers of the Maginot Line. The Germans watched them and did nothing.

On 3 September, the day war was declared, Winston Churchill – a long-time opponent of the policy of appeasement – returned to government ranks as First Lord of the Admiralty. It was a post he had been holding when the First World War was declared twenty-five years before. Legend states that the signal 'Winston is back' was sent to all ships of the fleet, although, with no copy of the message remaining, the veracity of the signal has lately been questioned.

That same day, in the North Atlantic, the liner *Athenia* was torpedoed and sunk by the U30. The *Athenia* was en route to Montreal, carrying 1,400 passengers, 300 of them Americans, and was the first British vessel to be sunk in the war. Ninety-eight passengers and nineteen crew were lost, some by the blast of the torpedo, others in the confusion of trying to abandon ship.

On his return to base, Fritz-Julius Lemp, the captain of the U30, claimed that he had mistaken the blacked-out liner on her zigzag course for an armed merchant cruiser, which would have been a legitimate target. Nobody believed a word of it.

The sinking of the *Athenia* brought howls of protest in Britain, Canada and neutral America. Totally embarrassed, the German government tried to blame the attack on the British themselves, stating that Churchill had ordered the sinking to marshal anti-German feelings in neutral countries. Such a patently ridiculous argument was never likely to work. Karl Dönitz himself ordered the entries regarding the sinking to be removed from U30's log.

Mistakes in identity were not uncommon in the early days of the war. On 5 September an RAF Anson bomber attacked two British submarines, thinking they were U-boats, scoring a direct hit on the conning tower of HMS *Snapper*.

Ten days later, the submarine *Oxley* was rammed and sunk by the *Triton*, the first British submarine to be lost in the war. As if that mishap was not enough, four days later the submarine *Sturgeon* narrowly missed sinking her sister ship *Swordfish*. They were the start of an ever-increasing casualty list as, in all, seventy-six British submarines were lost during the war.

On 5 September the *Royal Sceptre*, an armed merchantman, was torpedoed by U48. As if to demonstrate that all courtesy and humanity had not yet disappeared from naval warfare, the U-boat then proceeded to stop another British ship, the SS *Browning*, to request that she pick up survivors from the sunken ship.

It was not all one-way traffic, however. On 14 September, the U39 was forced to the surface and then sunk by the destroyers *Faulkner*, *Firedrake* and *Foxhound* off the Hebrides while she was attempting to attack the aircraft carrier *Ark Royal*. The carrier was unharmed, and the depth charges of the three escorts did their job quite efficiently. It was the first U-boat loss of the war.

By 1939, aircraft carriers had assumed a vitally important role in the operations of any major surface fleet. As such, they were obvious targets for submarines, and on 17 September the first significant warship sinking of the war occurred when the carrier *Courageous* was torpedoed in the Western Approaches. Engaged in convoy protection duties, the *Courageous* was spotted by Otto Schuhart in U29, but the U-boat could not surface either to attack or pursue the carrier, because of aircraft activity overhead.

Despite her slow speed – the U-boat could manage only 8 knots while submerged – Schuhart shadowed the carrier for two hours. As he later wrote, 'We were told during our training to always stay close and that is exactly what I did.'

Gradually, U29 began to lose ground on the carrier but then *Audacious* turned into the wind to fly off aircraft, and presented Schuhart with a perfect side-on view. Two torpedoes struck home from less than 3,000 yards. The aircraft carrier turned onto her side and was torn apart by two huge internal explosions. She sank in less than 15 minutes, taking 519 men down with her.

The U29 was immediately attacked by the British escorts, but dived deep – so deep that Schuhart thought her hull would crack. The attack went on for hours and only finally ended when the destroyers ran out of depth charges. Apart from the loss of a capital ship, the long-term effect of the sinking was significant, as the Royal Navy promptly withdrew the three remaining fleet aircraft carriers from the Western Approaches. It was an action that left convoys with no air cover.

The Fleet Air Arm was active in the opening days of the war, and on 26 September Lt McEwen in a Blackburn Skua from 803 Squadron, Fleet Air Arm, shot down the first German aircraft to be destroyed in the war. That same day the Germans claimed to have bombed and destroyed the *Ark Royal* – Göring even went as far as to decorate the pilot who claimed the success. As it transpired, the *Ark Royal* was then in the South Atlantic, hunting for the surface raider *Admiral Graf Spee*.

A few days later, on 30 September, the *Graf Spee* began her campaign of commerce raiding by sinking her first victim, the SS *Clement*. Having been deployed to the South Atlantic before war broke out, the *Graf Spee* was to wage a lonely campaign that saw her sink over 50,000 tons of Allied shipping during the coming months.

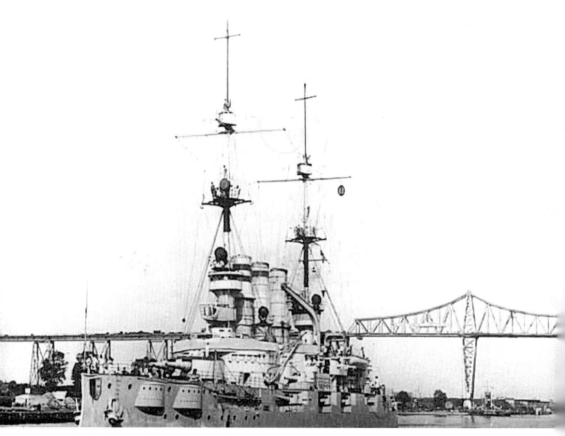

The first shots of the war were fired by the old First World War vintage battleship *Schleswig Holstein*, a Kriegsmarine training ship. It signalled the start of the German assault on Poland, and within days the world was at war. The *Schleswig Holstein*, like the rest of the German Navy, took almost no further part in the invasion of Poland, but she had at least fired her guns in anger.

Opposite page: On 3 September 1939, Neville Chamberlain's ultimatum for Germany to remove her troops from Poland ran out. With German troops still operating in the country and showing no inclination to retire, war was declared by Britain and France, a mere twenty-one years after the conclusion of the last one. Winston Churchill – so long in the political wilderness during the 1930s – returned to government as First Lord of the Admiralty. It was a position he relished, and one that gave him the chance to take a 'hands-on' role in the conflict.

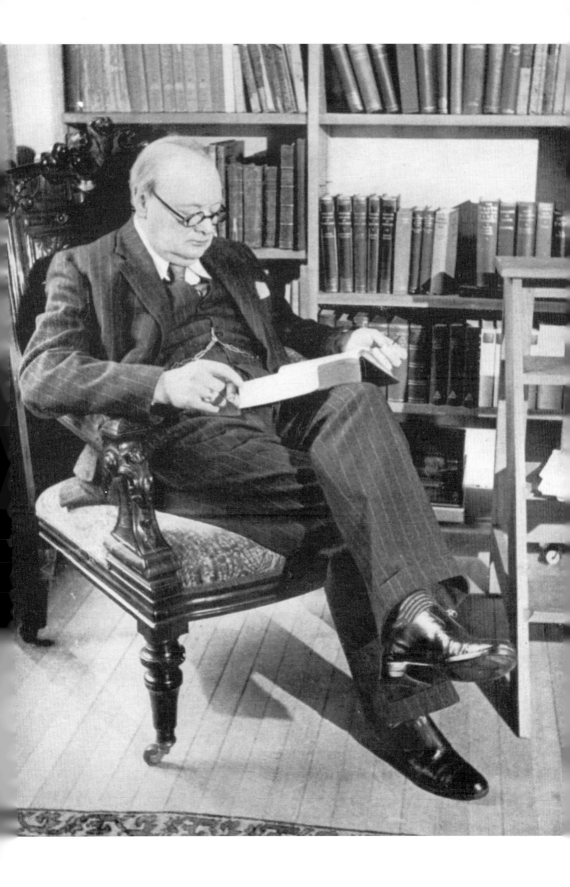

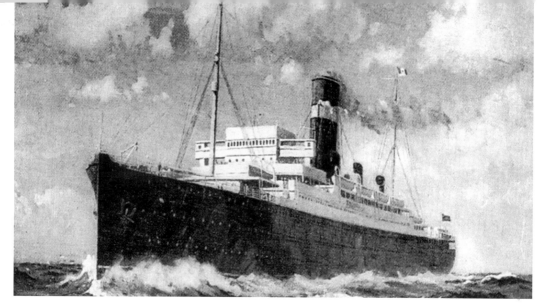

The first British casualty of the war at sea came the day war broke out. Out in the NW Approaches, the Donaldson liner *Athenia*, captained by James Cook, was torpedoed without warning by the U30. *Athenia* took fourteen hours to sink and, despite the assistance of numerous vessels, over ninety people went down with her. The Germans claimed they thought she was an armed merchant cruiser, but the fact that U30 had been tracking the liner for over three hours rather made a mockery of this claim – as did other statements that insisted the liner had been sunk by the British themselves and the blame conveniently laid at the door of Germany.

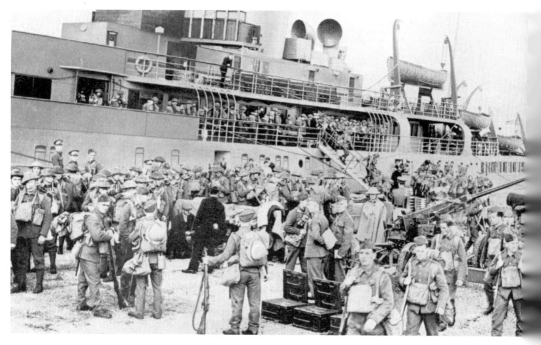

Starting on 10 September, transporting Lord Gort and the British Expeditionary Force to France became one of the early jobs of the Navy. It was hard, unglamorous work but something that had to be done if Britain was to honour her treaty obligations. The task was completed by 7 October. This view shows men of the BEF disembarking from their transport at one of the French Channel ports.

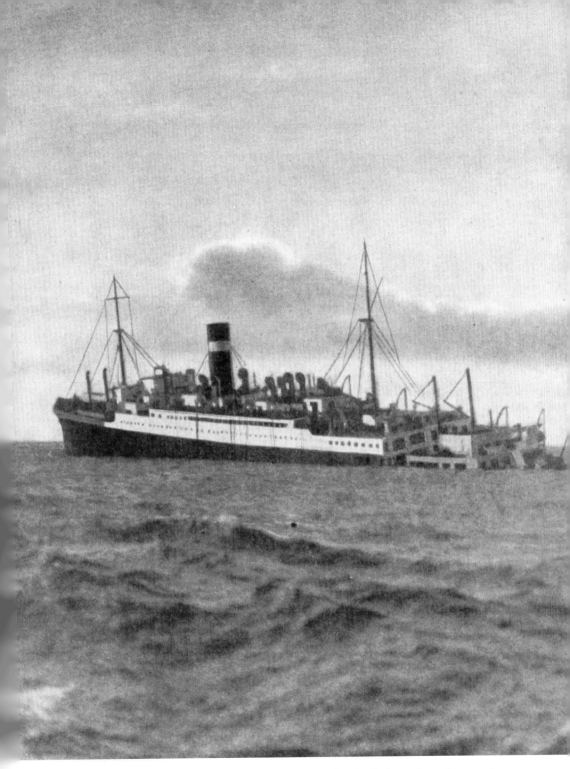

The *Athenia*, sinking slowly by the stern, is caught here in her death throes by a photographer on one of the attendant ships.

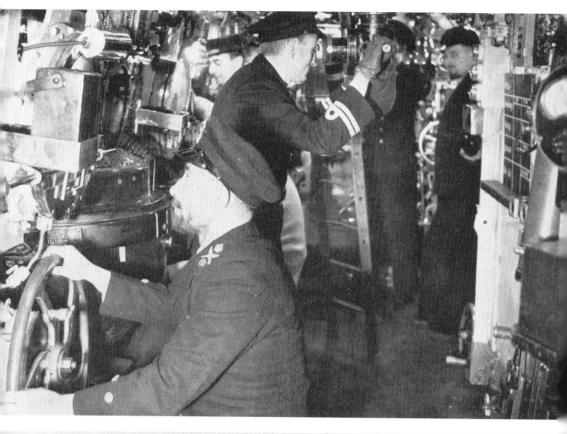
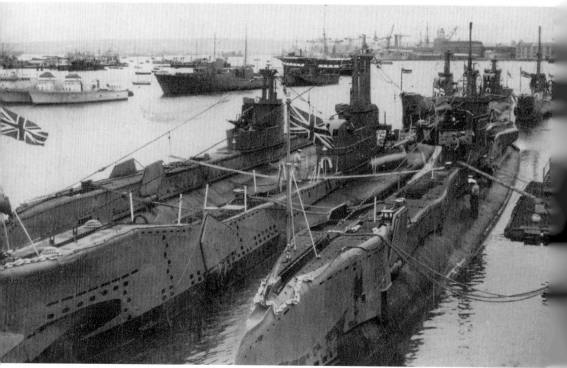

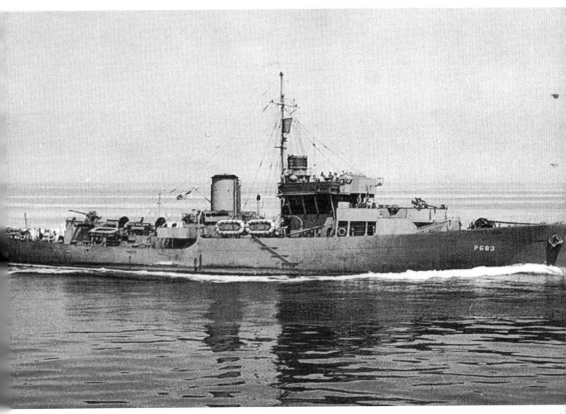

Depth charges had proved their worth in the First World War, and it was not long before the Royal Navy was employing old destroyers and new Flower Class corvettes (as in the picture above) – little more than big trawlers – to hurl these explosive charges at enemy submarines. The series of drawings on the following page, taken from *The Illustrated London News*, was published in the first year of the war, and gave the public some idea about how the weapon worked.

Opposite top: On 10 September the submarine *Oxley* became the first of seventy-six British submarines lost during the war. She was sunk by 'friendly fire' – she was actually rammed – from the *Triton*, something of an occupational hazard in these early days of the conflict. Life in a submarine was cramped and uncomfortable. It was also decidedly dangerous, and the men who sailed them, on both sides of the conflict, soon became a breed apart.

Opposite bottom: Submarines had shown their value in the First World War. In the interwar years, Britain had built many of these hidden craft so that when war broke out in 1939 the Royal Navy's submarine fleet was, at least, on a par with that of Germany. It was not to last, and Germany's intense U-boat programme soon outstripped that of Britain. This view shows Royal Navy submarines in port just before the outbreak of war.

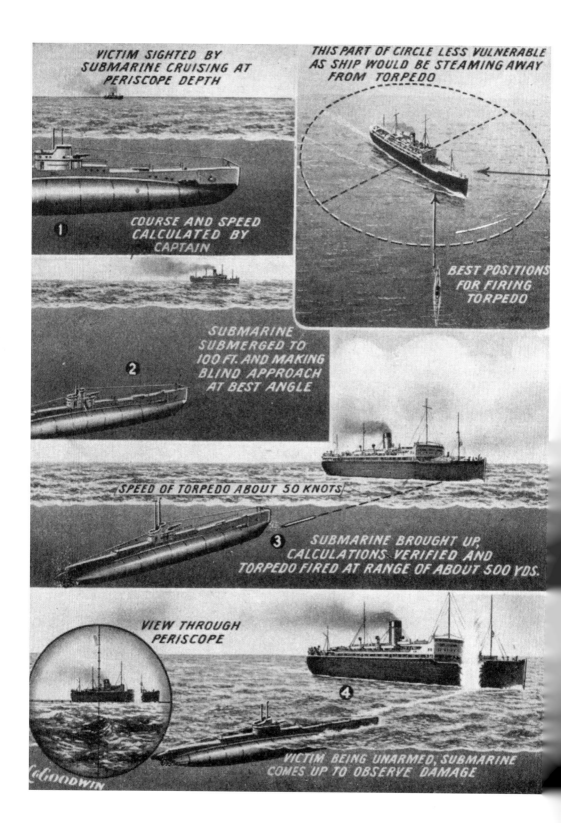

VICTIM SIGHTED BY SUBMARINE CRUISING AT PERISCOPE DEPTH

THIS PART OF CIRCLE LESS VULNERABLE AS SHIP WOULD BE STEAMING AWAY FROM TORPEDO

1 COURSE AND SPEED CALCULATED BY CAPTAIN

BEST POSITIONS FOR FIRING TORPEDO

2 SUBMARINE SUBMERGED TO 100 FT. AND MAKING BLIND APPROACH AT BEST ANGLE

SPEED OF TORPEDO ABOUT 50 KNOTS

3 SUBMARINE BROUGHT UP, CALCULATIONS VERIFIED AND TORPEDO FIRED AT RANGE OF ABOUT 500 YDS.

VIEW THROUGH PERISCOPE

4 VICTIM BEING UNARMED, SUBMARINE COMES UP TO OBSERVE DAMAGE

GoGoodwin

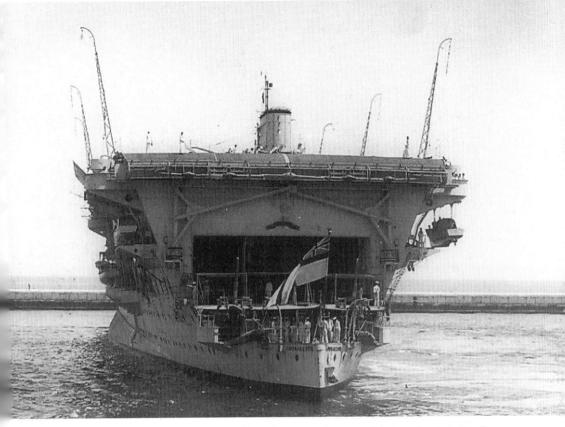

Coasters, trawlers and merchant ships had been lost since day one of the war, but Britain's first major warship loss of the conflict came when the aircraft carrier *Courageous* was torpedoed and sunk by U29 on 17 September. The *Courageous* was engaged in convoy escort duty at the time of the attack and cruising at a relatively slow speed. Despite this, and after following the carrier for several hours, the U-boat was beginning to fall behind until the *Courageous* turned into the wind to fly off aircraft and presented a wonderful target for the hidden submarine. Two torpedoes were fired, one struck.

Opposite page: The U-boat threat both fascinated and appalled the British public, who found newspaper accounts of the sinkings compelling reading. Things changed later in the war when the attacks reached epidemic heights, but in these early days papers and magazines gleefully printed articles and diagrams showing how U-boats operated.

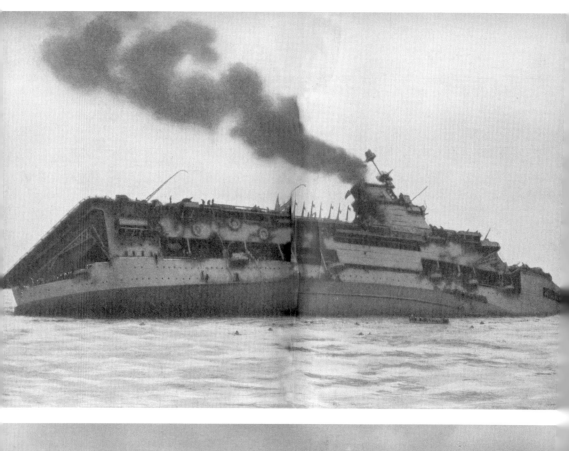

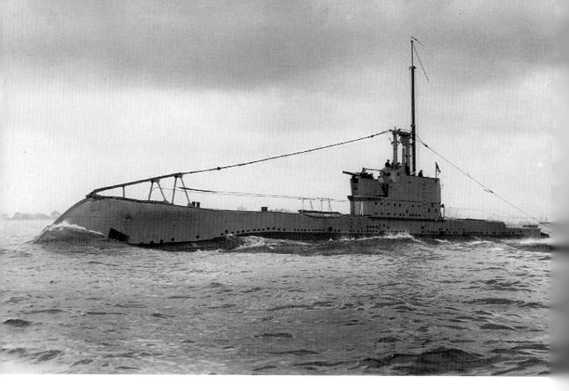

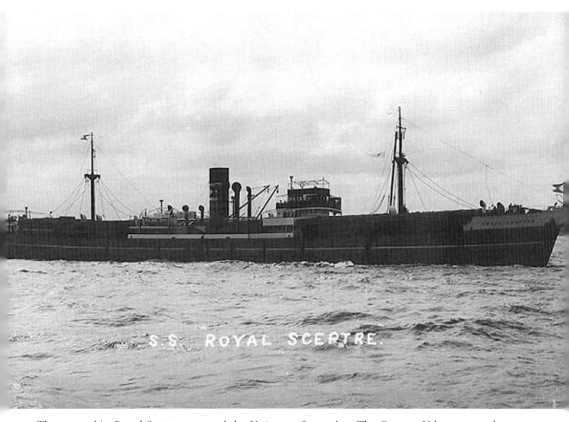

The cargo ship *Royal Sceptre* was sunk by U48 on 5 September. The German U-boat stopped another British ship to ask her to pick up the survivors – such humanity did not last long.

Opposite top: The *Courageous* sank in just 15 minutes, with huge loss of life. Forty-eight valuable aircraft were also lost. U29 dived deep, so deep her captain feared the hull would crack, and hugged the bottom of the sea. Despite being repeatedly depth charged by the escorting destroyers, the U-boat survived the attacks and returned to base. The sinking frightened those in charge at the Admiralty, with the result that aircraft carriers – already the most valuable ships of war in the fleet – were removed from the Western Approaches for several years. Aircraft, arguably one of the most effective ways of dealing with the U-boat threat, were thus largely denied the convoys.

Opposite bottom: The submarine *Oxley*, rammed and sunk by the *Triton* in September 1939. She was the first submarine loss of the war.

October

On 8 October, Captain Günther Prien sailed out of Kiel in U47, his intention being to carry out a daring raid on the British fleet anchorage at Scapa Flow.

A day later, the brand-new heavy cruiser *Belfast* captured the *Cap Norte* off the Faroe Islands, and brought her into port. The German vessel was renamed *Empire Trooper* and put into service with the Navy.

By the evening of 13 October, Prien and U47 had arrived off the Scottish coast. A few hours later they managed to thread their way through British boom defences and enter Scapa Flow, where, despite being on the surface, the U-boat remained undetected for several hours. Then, early in the morning of 14 October, Prien fired the first of his torpedoes at the battleship *Royal Oak*, which was lying, unsuspecting, at anchor.

Amazingly there was no reaction from shore defences when the first torpedo struck the *Royal Oak*'s bow, and Prien, hardly believing his luck, readjusted his position and calmly reloaded for another attack. Three more torpedoes were fired, and soon huge explosions erupted on board the battleship. She sank swiftly, taking 883 sailors with her, as Prien headed back out to sea and home. The attack cruelly exposed weaknesses in the British defence system – by an ironic twist of fate, the blockships that had been ordered for the anchorage arrived a day after the disaster.

Three days later, Günther Prien and his crew arrived back at Kiel to a welcome fit for heroes. Admiral Raeder promoted Dönitz to Rear Admiral on the deck of the U-boat while Prien and his crew were flown to Berlin for decorations from Hitler himself and for more celebrations.

Scapa Flow was again in the wars on 17 October when the aged battleship *Iron Duke* – Jellicoe's flagship at the Battle of Jutland – was bombed during a German attack. The ship was damaged and had to be grounded. However, she remained in commission. On the 21st of the month the armed merchant cruiser *Transylvania*, part of the Northern Patrol that was implementing a blockade of German ports, sank the converted surface raider *Poseidon* in the sea off Iceland.

By the end of October, both Britain and Germany had laid thousands of magnetic mines around the entrances to ports and on the major shipping routes. The mine now became a significant weapon, accounting for many tons of shipping during the war years. The beginnings of the British Channel Mine Barrage had been laid between the Goodwin Sands and Dunkirk as early as 16 September, and the first German magnetic mine was exploded by minesweepers operating in the Bristol Channel off Swansea on 20 October.

During October, four German U-boats were damaged or disabled while trying to pass through the English Channel. It forced Dönitz to order that, in future, any U-boat heading for the Atlantic must make the journey around the north of Scotland rather than take the quicker but clearly more dangerous passage through the Channel.

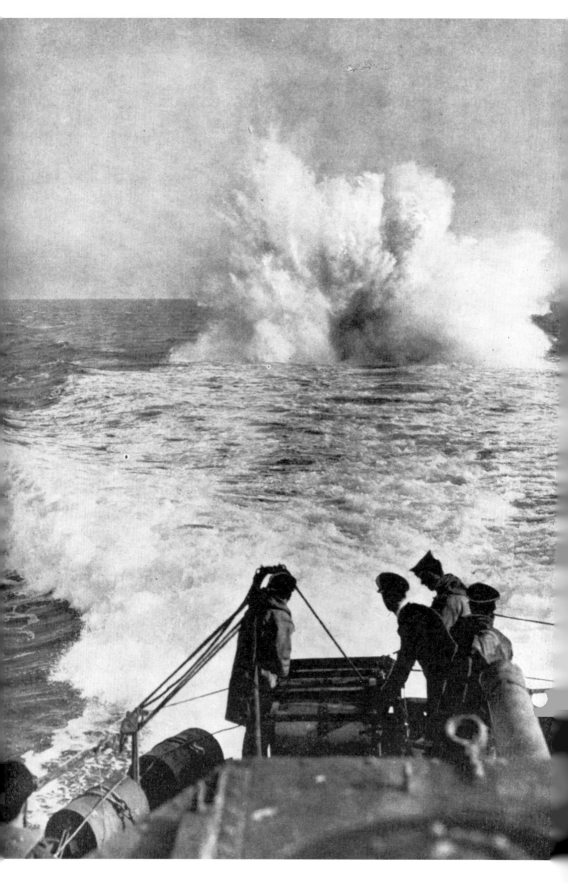

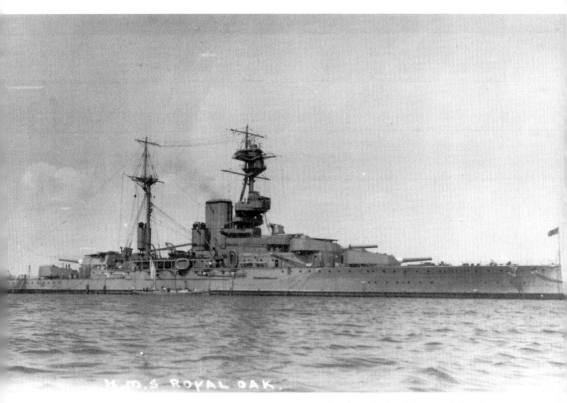

On the night of 13 October, Günther Prien and U47 managed to breach the defences of the Fleet Anchorage at Scapa Flow in the Orkneys. The Germans could hardly believe their luck and, having managed to slip through the barrage at the mouth of the anchorage, spent much of the night on the surface, waiting for the right moment to attack. That moment came in the early morning of the 14th when Prien fired his torpedoes at the battleship *Royal Oak*.

Opposite page: The German U-boat offensive continued unabated throughout the early months of the war, although, in compliance with the Hague Convention, most attacks only took place after warnings from the submarine. Such courtesies were not reciprocated by the British; when they encountered enemy submarines they immediately attacked, as this newspaper photograph clearly shows.

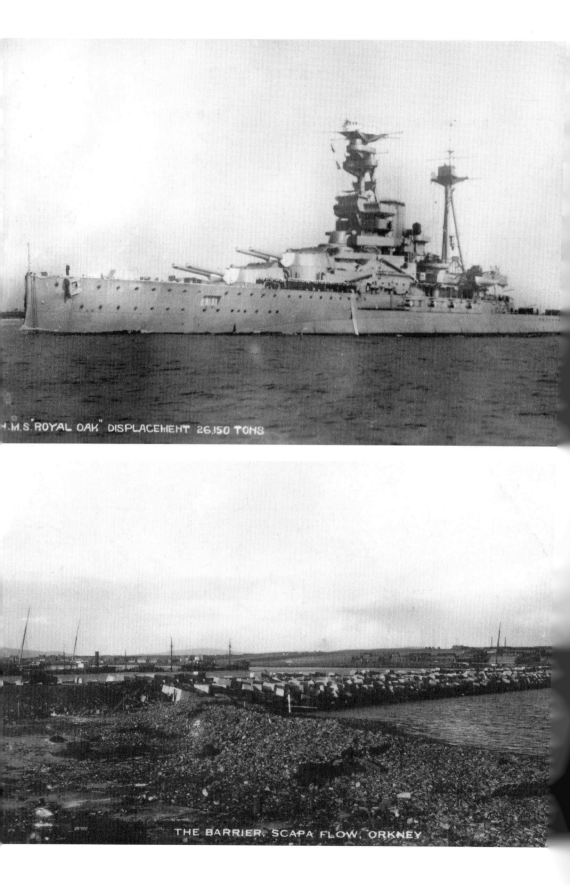

H.M.S. "ROYAL OAK" DISPLACEMENT 26,150 TONS

THE BARRIER, SCAPA FLOW, ORKNEY

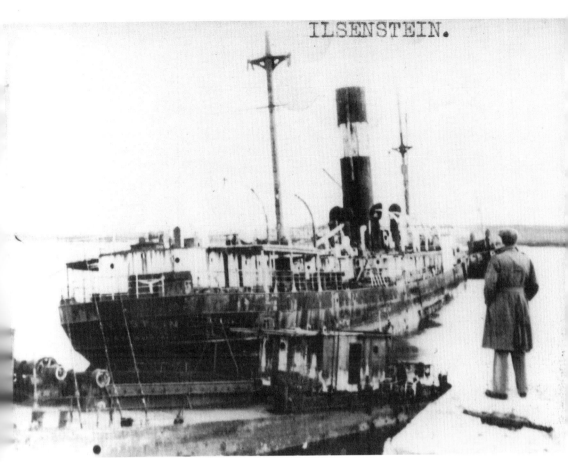

ILSENSTEIN.

On their return to base, Prien and his crew were decorated and treated like heroes. Admiral Raeder promoted Karl Dönitz, who had come to Wilhelmshaven to welcome back the submarine, to rear admiral on the deck of U47. The crew were even flown to Berlin for a special reception, where Prien was awarded the Knight's Cross, and officers and men met Adolf Hitler. For the British, however, the disaster showed the defensive inadequacies of Scapa Flow. Tragically, the blockships that had been sent for to make the defences more secure arrived the day after the sinking.

Opposite top: Prien's first torpedo, which struck the battleship on her bow, did only limited damage, but, to his amazement, it also did very little to attract attention. Consequently he fired again, and this time the *Royal Oak* was struck amidships. The ship exploded in a ball of flame and sank, taking over 800 men with her. The Admiralty and the public were horrified that such an attack could take place inside Scapa Flow, the anchorage of the Home Fleet.

Opposite bottom: The Scapa Flow barrage, designed to protect the anchorage from attacks like that by Günther Prien.

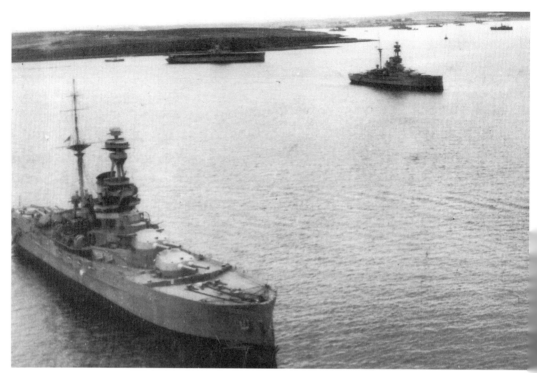

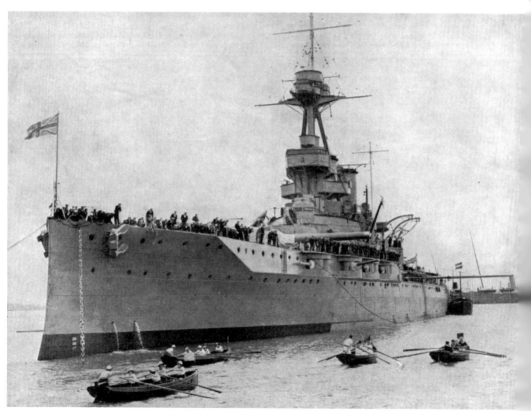

34

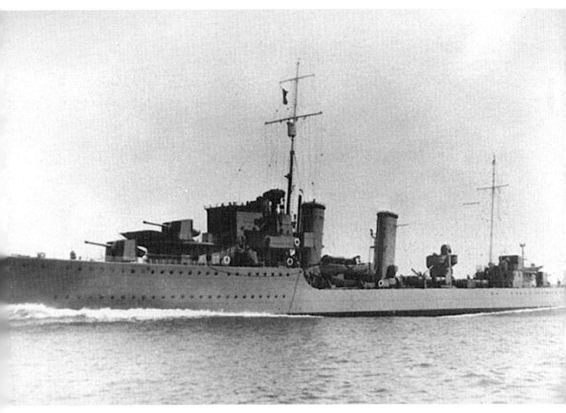

The *Ilex*, which, along with the *Imogen*, sank the U42 in the Western Approaches on 13 October.

Opposite top: One way of defending the anchorage at Scapa Flow was creating 'dummy ships', decoy vessels that were built up to look like real capital ships, battlecruisers and the like. This photograph shows a dummy R Class battleship and an aircraft carier sitting in the anchorage – the real ships were elsewhere.

Opposite bottom: The *Iron Duke*, Jellicoe's flagship at Jutland, was damaged in an aerial attack on 17 October 1939. She was grounded but remained in service.

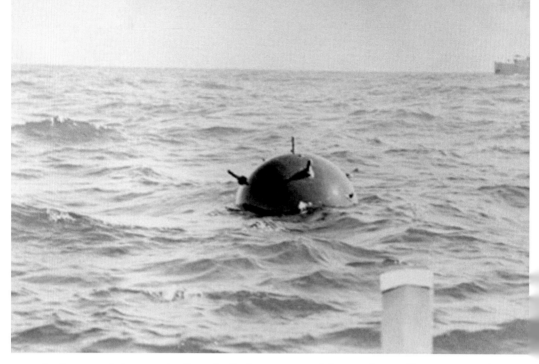

A mine, one of the most deadly and effective weapons of the war. In an effort to protect the British coast, the Channel mine barrage was laid and in place by 16 October 1939.

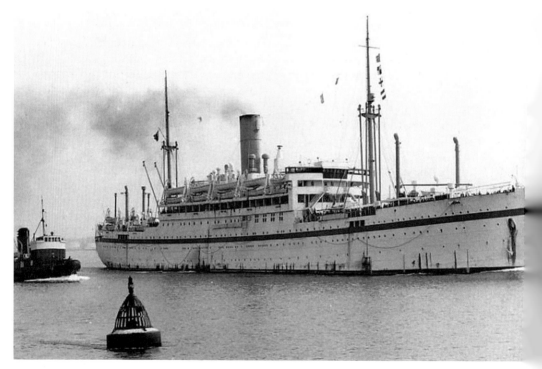

The *Empire Trooper*. Formerly the German cargo vessel *Cap Norte*, she was captured by the *Belfast* on 9 October, taken into port and commissioned into the Merchant Marine.

November

On the first day of November, the pocket battleship *Deutschland* returned to port after a frustrating and fruitless cruise in the waters off Greenland and Iceland. Two weeks later, Adolf Hitler, conscious of the potential blow to morale should any vessel bearing Germany's name happen to be sunk, renamed the ship *Lutzow*.

On 13 November, while escorting the minelayer *Adventure*, the destroyer *Blanche* struck a magnetic mine in the Thames Estuary. She was the first of 139 British destroyers lost during the war. A few days later, another destroyer, the *Gipsy*, also became a mine victim, while, on 21 November, the cruiser *Belfast* was severely damaged by a magnetic mine in the Firth of Forth.

British successes in November were limited, but on the 18th of the month the armed merchant cruiser *California*, patrolling off Iceland, captured two German cargo vessels, the *Borkum* and *Eilbek*. The *California* was one of fifty-five merchantmen and liners converted into ships of war by the British during the Second World War. Fifteen of them were sunk before they were finally withdrawn from service in the North Atlantic.

Two days after the *California*'s success, HMS *Sturgeon* sank the German trawler *Telschau* 30 miles north of Heligoland. It was the first British submarine victory of the war.

On 23 November, the armed merchant cruiser *Rawalpindi* sighted the German battlecruisers *Scharnhorst* and *Gneisenau* to the north of the Faroes. The German ships were attempting to break out through the defensive screen of patrolling British vessels and sortie into the Atlantic to attack Allied shipping. Despite being totally outgunned, Captain E. C. Kennedy immediately radioed the position of the enemy ships and went in to attack.

The *Rawalpindi* managed to score several hits on the *Scharnhorst* before the battlecruiser's heavy guns began to take their toll. Blazing furiously, the *Rawalpindi* was soon disabled and sunk. The German ships, their presence now known to the Admiralty, returned to port without causing damage to British trade.

The cruiser *Newcastle*, which was the next ship in the patrol screen, managed to pick up eleven survivors from the *Rawalpindi*, the *Scharnhorst* a few dozen more, but Captain Kennedy was not among them.

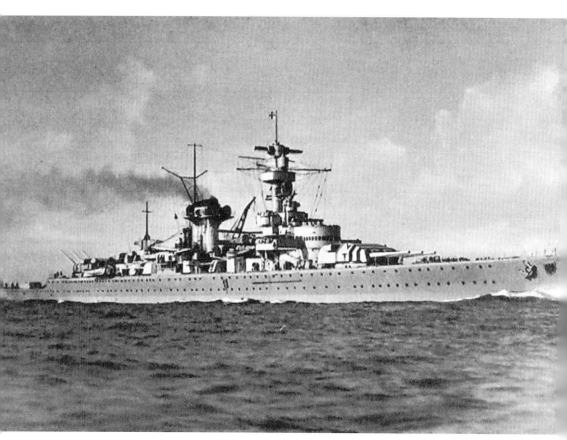

The pocket battleship *Deutschland* was always more of a liability than a benefit to the Kriegsmarine. This was not so much because of her power, which, like that of the *Graf Spee*, was immense, but more about her name. The potential humiliation of any ship bearing the name of the country being sunk by enemy action was more than Adolf Hitler could bear, and in early November he insisted that her name be changed to *Lutzow*.

Opposite page: The advantage of commerce raiders had been shown by Admiral von Spee and his ships of the East Asiatic Squadron in the First World War. His namesake, the pocket battleship *Admiral Graf Spee*, had been sent to the Southern Atlantic before war broke out, and soon she began sinking British and Allied merchant ships. The valuable cargoes of these ships were sometimes purloined by the *Graf Spee* but equally as often they went, with the ships themselves, to the bottom of the ocean.

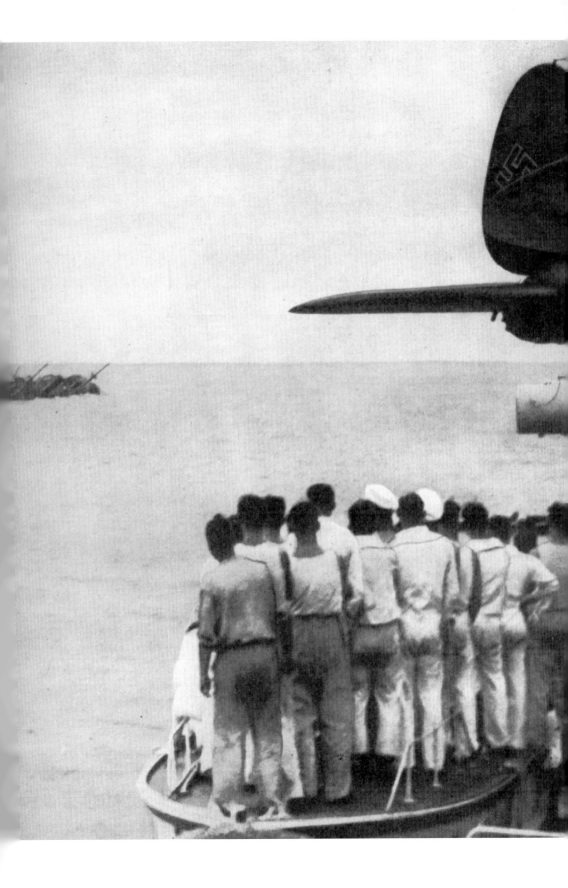

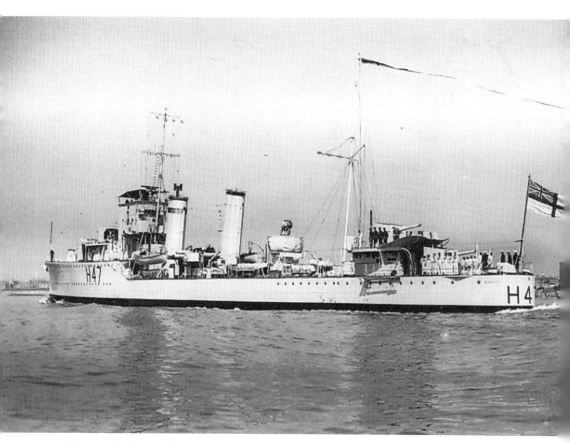

The *Blanche* became the first British destroyer to be sunk in the war, when, on 13 November, she struck a magnetic mine in the Thames Estuary. In a moment of sheer black comedy, the destroyer was actually escorting the minelayer *Advantage* at the time. The *Blanche* foundered quickly. All told, 139 destroyers, the workhorses of the Navy, were lost by the Royal Navy in the six years of conflict.

Opposite page: The dubious art of laying mines had moved on since the First World War when the weapons had been dropped from ships. Now, surface vessels, submarines and even aircraft were used to lay mines, as this article from 1939 clearly shows.

40

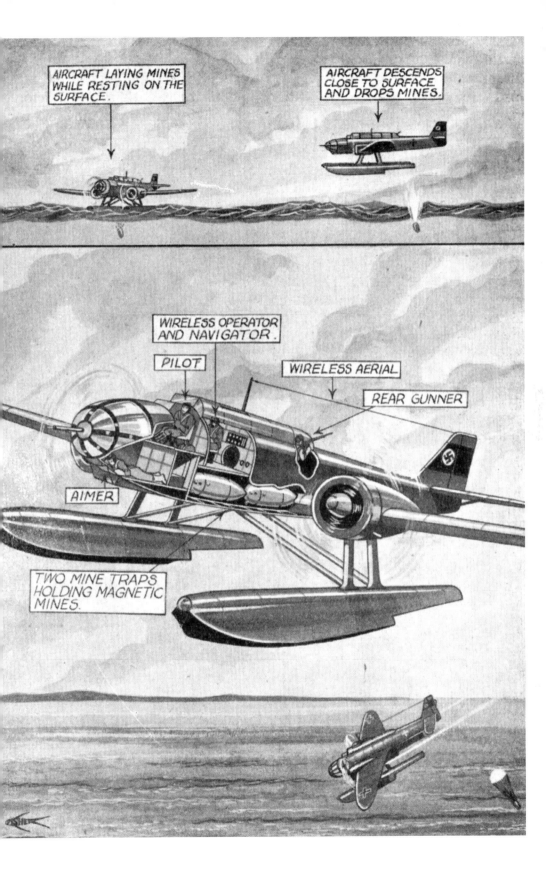

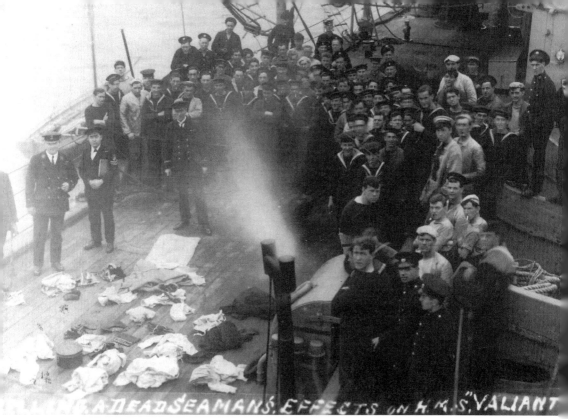

SELLING A DEAD SEAMAN'S EFFECTS ON H.M.S. "VALIANT"

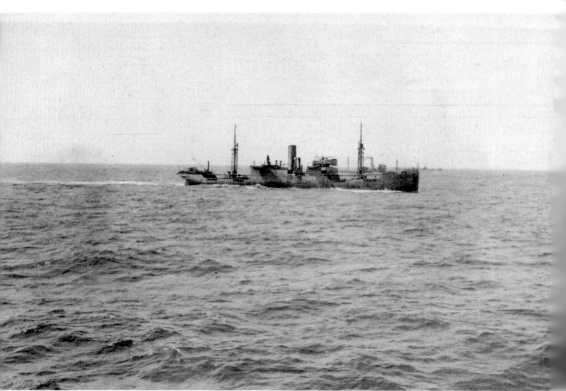

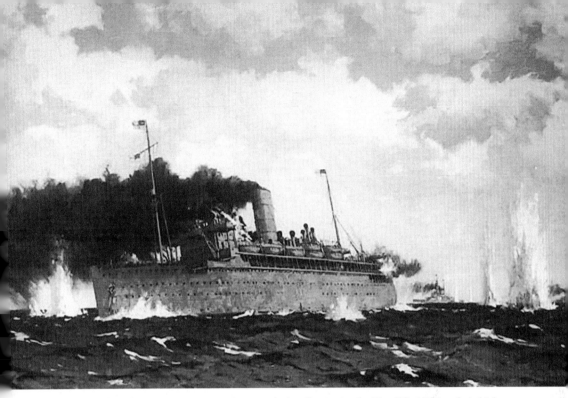

Armed merchant cruisers had not proved particularly effective in the First World War, their high freeboard and lack of armour making them particularly vulnerable to anything other than ships of the same type or class. Nevertheless, AMCs were commissioned again in this war, fifty-five of them being used and fifteen sunk before they were finally withdrawn. On 23 November, the AMC *Rawalpindi*, operating as part of the Northern Patrol and commanded by Captain E. C. Kennedy, came into contact with the German battlecruisers *Scharnhorst* and *Gneisenau*, which were attempting to break out into the Atlantic.

Opposite top: Life goes on. Despite wartime conditions, life in the Royal Navy, with all its traditions like a daily tot of rum and sailors sleeping in hammocks, continued much as normal. This photograph shows another of those traditions, the selling off of a dead sailor's possessions on board the battleship *Valiant*.

Opposite bottom: On 17 November 1939 the U-boats were finally given permission to attack, out of hand, any vessel they thought might be British or French. Previously, any cargo ships that the U-boat commanders suspected of being from Germany's enemies were meant to be stopped and examined before being sunk. This had not always happened, but now Dönitz's order meant that lone merchant vessels suddenly became particularly vulnerable.

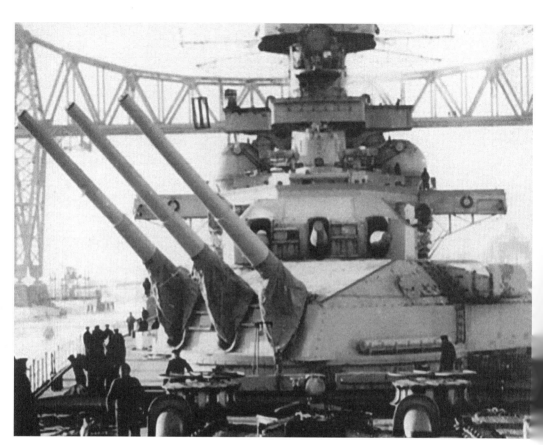

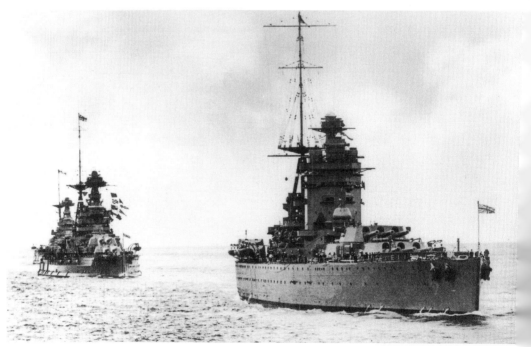

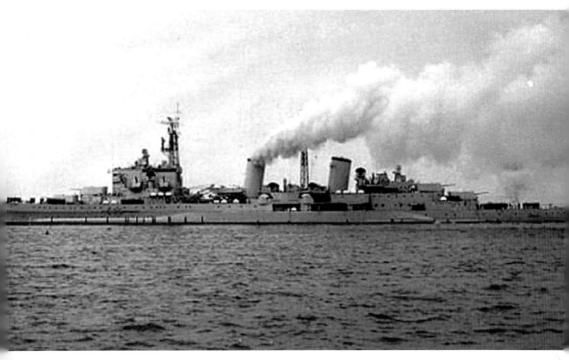

The new heavy cruiser *Belfast*, severely damaged by a mine in the Firth of Forth on 21 November 1939.

Opposite top: After radioing his position, Kennedy attacked. It was always a hopeless action. The *Rawalpindi* was struck repeatedly by shells from the *Scharnhorst* before heeling over and sinking. Only eleven survivors were picked up, but the two German battlecruisers, their position now known to the British, promptly returned to port. Kennedy and the *Rawalpindi* had not died in vain, as the two German ships could have caused untold havoc out in the Atlantic. The massive 11-inch guns of the *Scharnhorst* are shown in this photograph; they are weapons that would have wreaked havoc on any convoy the ship encountered.

Opposite bottom: Britain's strength lay in its battle fleet. Despite many of the giant warships being old and, compared to German vessels like the *Bismarck* and *Scharnhorst*, somewhat slow and under-armoured, it was still a powerful fighting force. Hitler knew he would have to defeat the Royal Navy if he was ever going to invade Britain, and with ships like the *Rodney* and *Barham*, shown here at sea before the war, that was never going to be likely.

December

December began badly for British naval forces when, on the 4th of the month, the battleship *Nelson* was severely damaged by a mine as she was entering Loch Ewe. She was put out of action for several months. On the 7th, British and German destroyers clashed for the first time in the North Sea. In a largely inconclusive action, the *Jersey* was hit and badly damaged by a German torpedo.

Some retribution came for the British on 13 December, when the submarine *Salmon* sighted two large warships about 100 miles west of Jutland. They turned out to be the German cruisers *Leipzig* and *Nürnberg*. The *Salmon* had, on 4 December, already sunk the U36, in the first successful submarine-on-submarine attack of the war, and now she closed on the two enemy cruisers.

Both cruisers were torpedoed, and were forced to limp back to base. The *Leipzig* took over a year to repair, and thereafter was relegated to training duties. *Nürnberg* was repaired in six months. Lt-Com. Bickford, the captain of the *Salmon*, was promoted and awarded the DSO for his actions during the hugely successful patrol.

Since the start of hostilities, the German raider *Graf Spee* had been fighting a lonely commerce-raiding war under the command of Karl Langsdorff in the South Atlantic. No one knew where she would turn up next, but early in the month Commodore Henry Harwood, stationed at the Falkland Islands with a force of three cruisers, picked up a radio message from the freighter *Doric Star*. The British cargo ship had been stopped by the *Graf Spee*, and managed to give her position off the coast of Africa before she was boarded and sunk by the German sailors.

Another cry for help, this time by the merchant ship *Tairoa*, enabled Harwood to plot, reasonably accurately, the course that *Graf Spee* was now taking. By Harwood's reckoning she would soon appear off the coast of South America and, consequently, he concentrated his three cruisers, *Ajax*, *Achilles* and *Exeter*, off the mouth of the River Plate, exactly where he thought Kapitän Langsdorff and his ship would soon appear.

On 13 December, Langsdorff spotted the smoke of the British cruisers and, mistaking it for the smoke of destroyers escorting a convoy, immediately steamed towards them. By the time he realised his mistake it was too late – he now had no option other than to fight.

The Battle of the River Plate was a hard and brutal contest. After two hours, both *Ajax* and *Exeter* had been badly hit by the shells from the *Graf Spee*, but the German raider had also suffered damage, and chose to break off the action.

Langsdorff made for neutral Montivideo, where he hoped he would be allowed to undertake vital repairs on his ship. *Exeter*, unable to continue, limped south towards the Falkland Islands while Harwood, with his two remaining cruisers, remained outside Montivideo, keeping the *Graf Spee* penned up in the neutral port.

Clever use of BBC radio broadcasts totally fooled Langsdorff into thinking that the carrier *Ark Royal* and battlecruiser *Renown* had joined Harwood and were waiting for him to emerge. In fact, the only reinforcement that had reached Harwood was the heavy cruiser *Cumberland*.

On 15 December, British sailors held by the *Graf Spee* were released to Uruguayan authorities, all of them commenting on the fair treatment they had received at the hands of Langsdorff and his crew. Nevertheless, in line with its position of neutrality, Uruguay insisted that the *Graf Spee* must leave harbour by 5.00 p.m. on 17 December.

Crewed by just forty sailors, the *Graf Spee* duly left Montivideo on the 17th, and came to a halt at the harbour entrance. There she was scuttled, explosive charges finishing the job, within sight and hearing of over 20,000 spectators who had come to witness the battle. The German government issued a statement that, unable to repair the *Graf Spee* in the time allowed, Langsdorff had no choice but to scuttle his ship once the Uruguayan ultimatum was given.

Kapitän Langsdorff probably disobeyed orders to engage the enemy ships and, believing he was faced by a markedly superior force, destroyed his own vessel rather than risk great loss of life. A man of some integrity, he then committed suicide on 20 December.

On 28 December, the battleship *Barham*, en route to join the Home Fleet, was torpedoed by U30 under the command of Fritz-Julius Lemp. It was the second mishap for the *Barham* that month as on 12 December she had collided with the destroyer *Duchess*, sinking the smaller vessel and killing 124 of her crew.

Two torpedoes were fired from U30, one of them being destroyed by the battleship's 'torpedo bulge'. The other caused considerable damage but, even so, *Barham* was able to make Liverpool under her own steam. She was out of service until April 1940.

The year 1939 came to a close with the German U-boat threat beginning to bite. In future, Germany declared, any vessel that was chartered to a British company or carrying goods to Britain, regardless of its nationality, would be sunk out of hand. The U-boat war was hotting up.

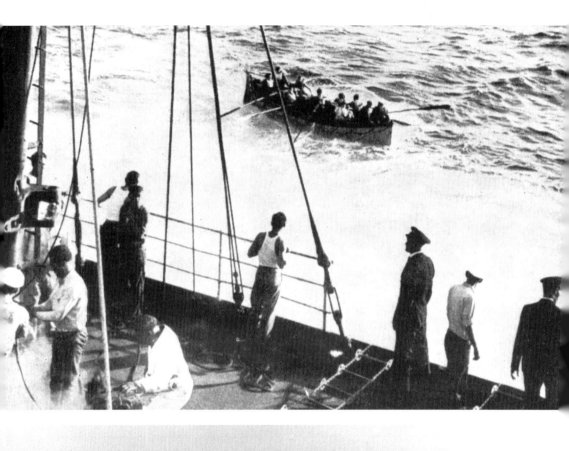
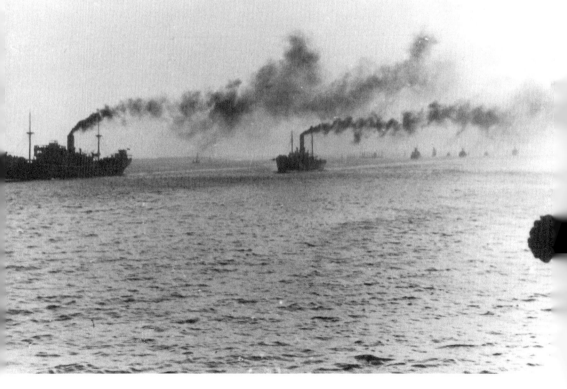

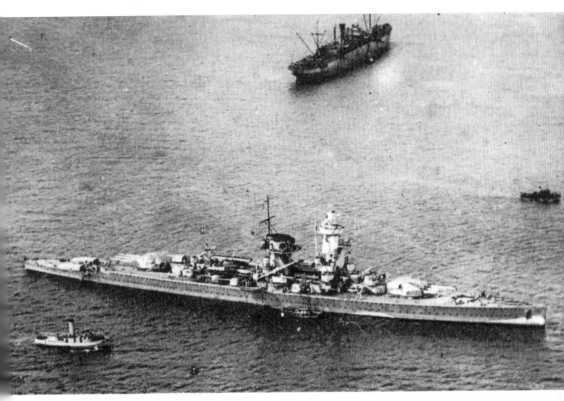

The Battle of the River Plate was the culmination of a four-month-long search for the raider *Graf Spee*, seen here in an aerial view while moored off Montevideo. Kapitän Hans Langsdorff, of the German pocket battleship, was a cool and calm character who knew how to do his job, but it was inevitable that, sooner or later, SOS messages from his victims would be picked up by the hunting British cruisers, messages that would reveal his whereabouts and the course he was taking. That was exactly what happened.

Opposite top: As 1939 drew to a close, German U-boat attacks continued. Tragically, many merchant seamen lost their lives, not in the U-boat attack but sitting in open lifeboats – sometimes for days on end – waiting for rescue. Unbelievably, the wages of these men were stopped immediately once their ships were sunk – hardly the most caring of attitudes from the shipowners.

Opposite bottom: Convoys were the only way to protect the lumbering merchant ships that brought in vital food supplies to Britain. The convoy system had worked effectively in 1917 and 1918 and, despite the lack of attention the anti-submarine arm of the Navy had been given between the wars, it was now beginning to be used again. German U-boat attacks had not yet reached the level of sophistication where coordinated Wolf Pack attacks could be made, but as early as November and December 1939 all sailors lived in fear of the sudden torpedo in the night. Ports like Glasgow, Liverpool and Milford Haven were, even at this early stage of the war, beginning to develop as convoy bases.

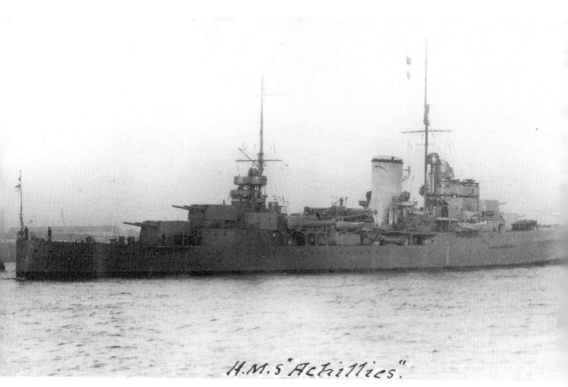

H.M.S "Achillies"

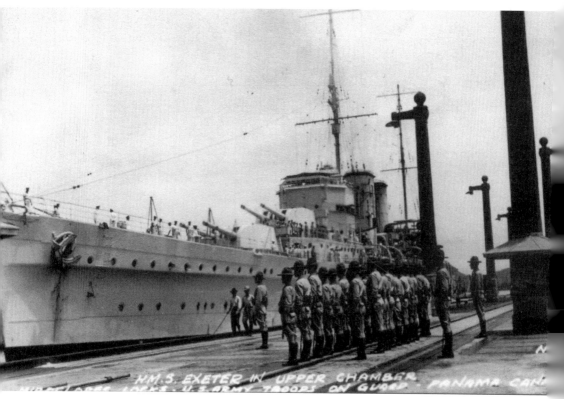

H.M.S. EXETER IN UPPER CHAMBER · PANAMA CAN
MIRAFLORES LOCKS. U.S. ARMY TROOPS ON GUARD

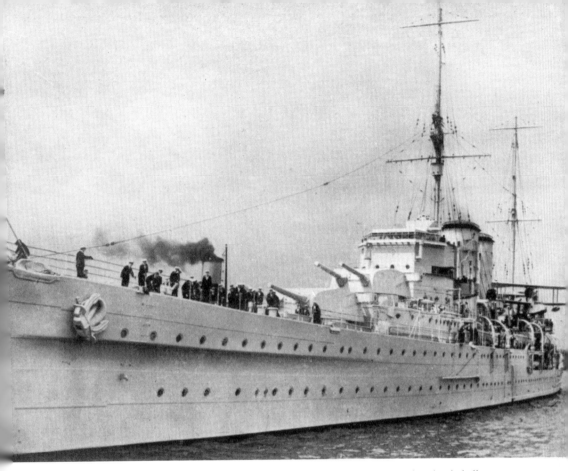

It was not all one-way traffic, however, and both *Ajax* and *Achilles* managed to land shells on the deck of the pocket battleship. The heavy armour plating of the battleship protected her from too much damage, but *Graf Spee* had been hunting merchantmen for several months; this was the first time she had encountered an enemy who was willing and able to hit back, and the effect unnerved the German crew. Dozens of British sailors, captured from the merchant ships she had sunk, were confined down below where they could hear the thud of shells hitting the *Graf Spee* and feel the shudder of the deck each time she fired.

Opposite top: On the morning of 13 December the *Graf Spee* ran head first into the three cruiser squadron of Commodore Henry Harwood off the coast of South America. Harwood, who was flying his pennant in the light cruiser *Ajax*, had plotted the course of the raider and despite the absence of the heavy cruiser *Cumberland*, then undergoing repairs at the Falkland Islands, was determined to bring Langsdorff to battle. Harwood's other ships included the heavy cruiser *Exeter* and the New Zealand ship *Achilles* (shown here).

Opposite bottom: The *Ajax*, *Achilles* and *Exeter* were outgunned by the *Graf Spee*, with her massive 11-inch armament, but nevertheless closed for action. At first, the Germans directed their fire onto the *Exeter*, which was soon badly hit and reeling away out of range. As the biggest of the British ships, *Exeter*'s 8-inch guns were a vital part of British firepower, but she was no match for the pocket battleship. With her effectively out of the battle, Langsdorff then switched his target to the *Ajax*. She, too, was hit many times.

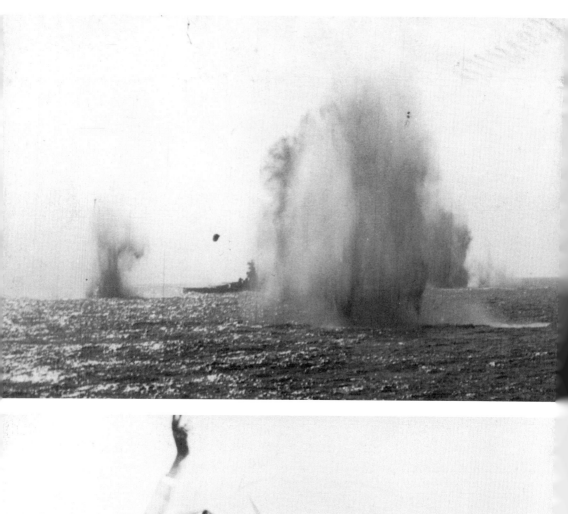

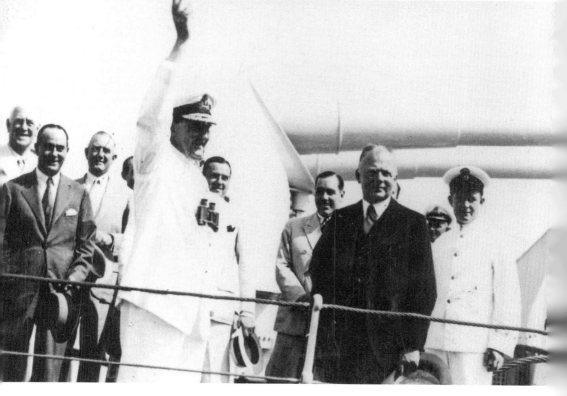

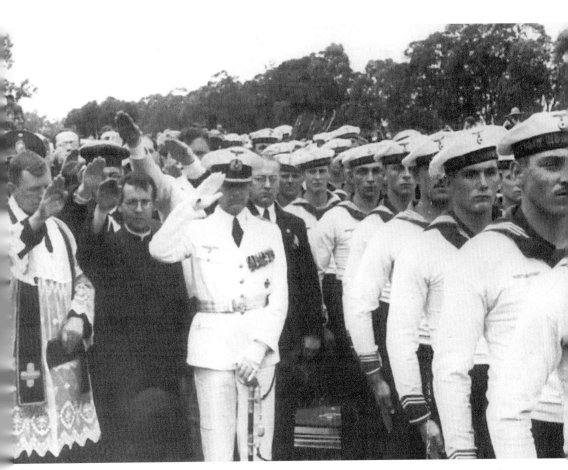

Clever use of radio broadcasts, and the careful spreading of false information, soon convinced Langsdorff that Harwood had been heavily reinforced by capital ships. These included, he was led to believe, the carrier *Ark Royal* – the thought of attack from carrier-borne Swordfish aircraft was not something he cared to contemplate for too long. Knowing that time was running out, Langsdorff buried his dead with full military honours. Interestingly, in the above photograph, taken at the burial service, Langsdorff is the only one to give the old-fashioned German naval salute. Everyone else, including the priests, uses the straight-armed Nazi salutation.

Opposite top: After an engagement that lasted over two hours, Langsdorff decided to break off the action. Why he should do this has never been totally clear, as the damage and casualties he had suffered were light enough and the three British ships were, if not exactly helpless, in no condition to cause him serious concern. Having made the decision to disengage, Langsdorff set a course for the neutral port of Montevideo.

Opposite bottom: Langsdorff's idea was to use the Uruguayan facilities at Montevideo to repair his ship, then venture out once more. Harwood and his battered cruisers remained outside territorial waters at the mouth of the River Plate, knowing that sooner or later the *Graf Spee* must emerge. By now, *Exeter* had limped off towards Port Stanley in the Falkland Islands, but the newly repaired *Cumberland* soon replaced her in Harwood's tiny force. The picture shows a jubilant Harwood on the deck of the *Ajax* in Montevideo after the battle.

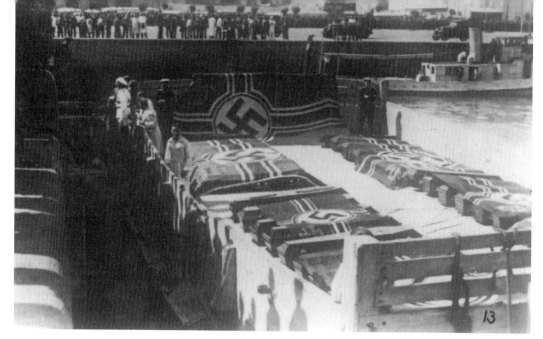

German dead are brought ashore from the damaged *Graf Spee*. An extension of stay in Montevideo was refused, and Langsdorff, given the news that he must leave port by the evening of 17 December, was faced with a terrible dilemma – fight, face internment or surrender. Hitler had ordered him to fight, to go down in a blaze of glory; but that would involve terrible loss of life, and Karl Langsdorff was too honourable a man for that.

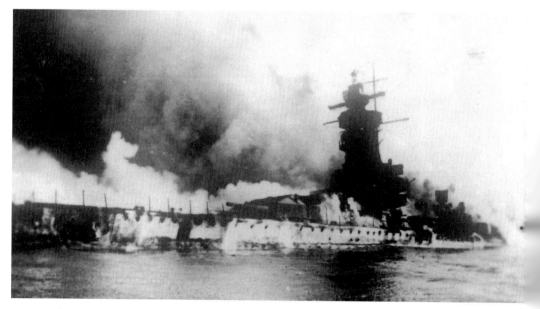

As the deadline of 17 December approached, the *Graf Spee* slowly left her moorings and headed out to sea. Just outside the harbour, she came to a halt and loud explosions were heard. Fires broke out and the battleship began to settle. Langsdorff had scuttled his once-proud ship rather than face the destruction he thought he would face outside Uruguayan territorial waters. The explosive charges planted by Langsdorff and his men totally destroyed the *Graf Spee*, which, blazing furiously, soon settled into the mud of the River Plate.

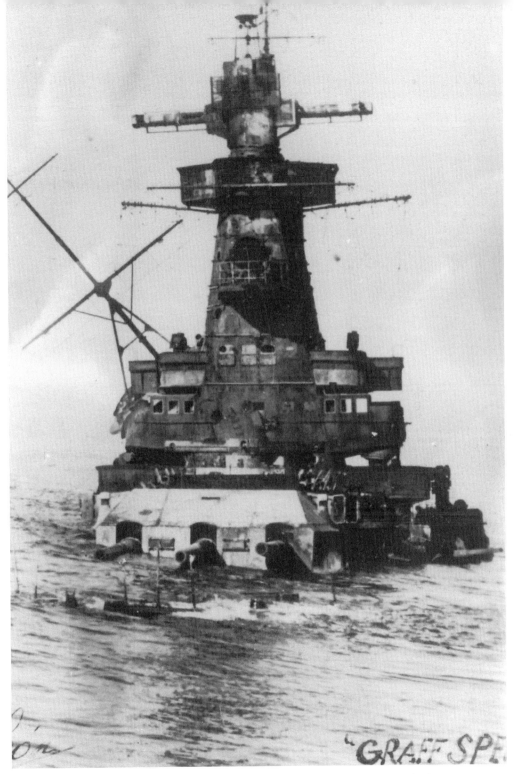

The sad remains of the *Graf Spee* lie in the shallow waters outside Montevideo harbour.

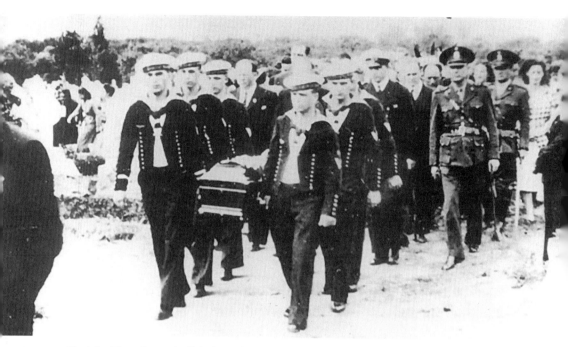

Kapitän Hans Langsdorff is buried in Montevideo. Three days after the destruction of his ship, Kapitän Langsdorff, proud and honourable to the last, shot himself in his hotel room in Montevideo. For Harwood and the British, there was the excitement and the glory of a famous victory against a bigger, stronger foe. It was the first major British success of the war, and Churchill at the Admiralty exploited it to the full.

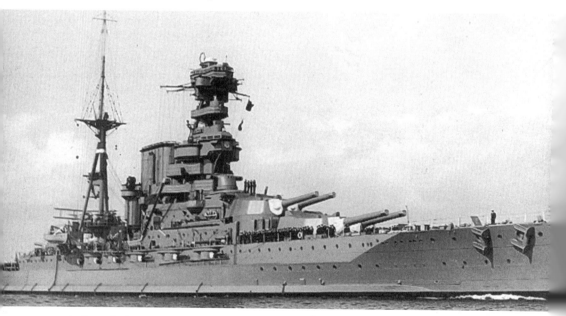

At the end of December, the battleship *Barham*, on her way to Scapa Flow, was torpedoed by U39 and seriously damaged. She managed to make it to port but the damage put her out of action for the next four months.

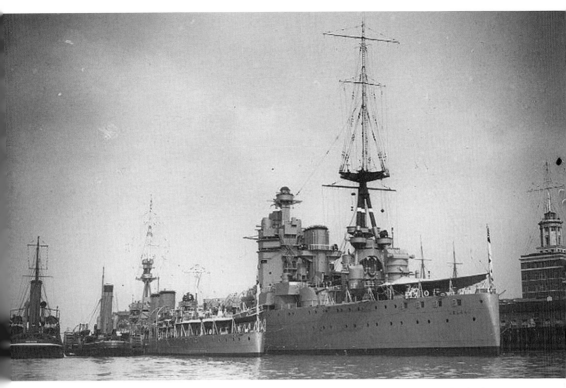

The massive battleship *Nelson*, all of her considerable armament mounted in front of the bridge. She was damaged by a mine on 13 December and put out of action for some weeks.

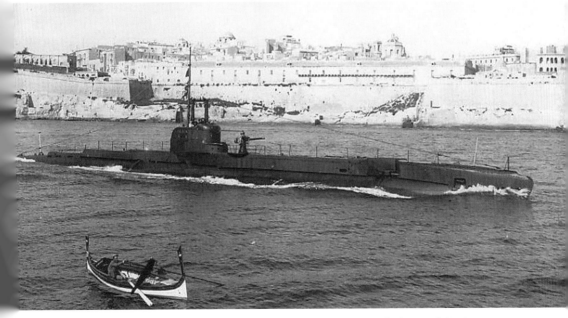

The submarine *Salmon*, which in December 1939 torpedoed and seriously damaged the German cruisers *Leipzig* and *Nürnberg*, is shown here in Malta.

General Navy Images

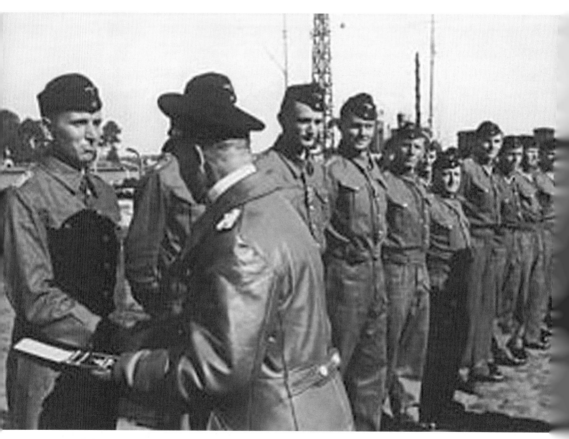

Admiral Raeder, head of the Kriegsmarine, congratulates U-boat ace Otto Krettschmer after another successful cruise.

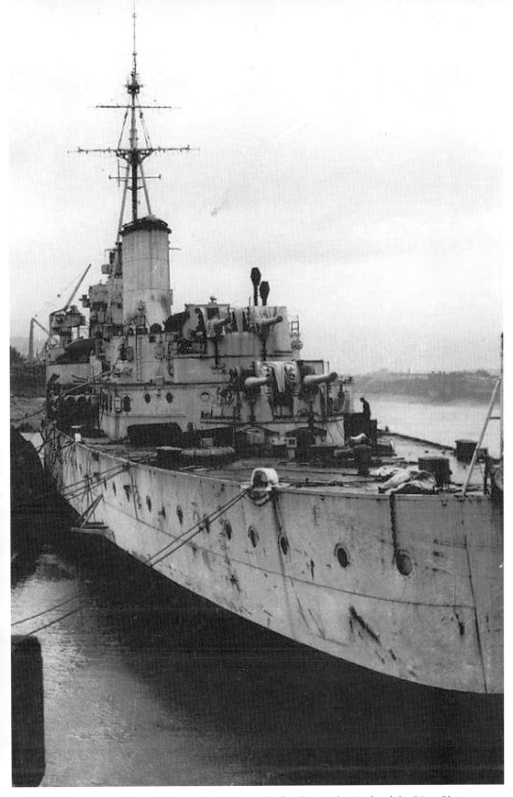

HMS *Ajax*, a stern view of Commodore Harwood's flagship at the Battle of the River Plate.

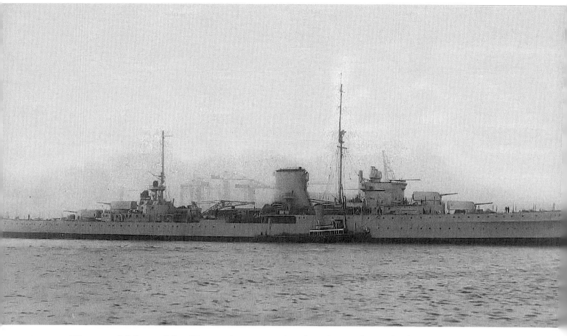

The graceful lines of the *Ajax* are best appreciated in this traditional side-on view. Her sister ship *Achilles* would have looked just the same.

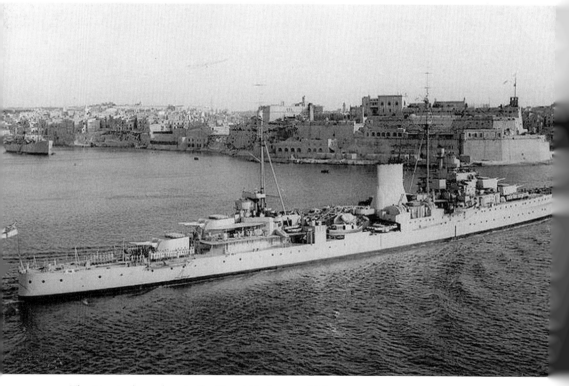

The *Ajax* is shown here in the Grand Harbour at Malta.

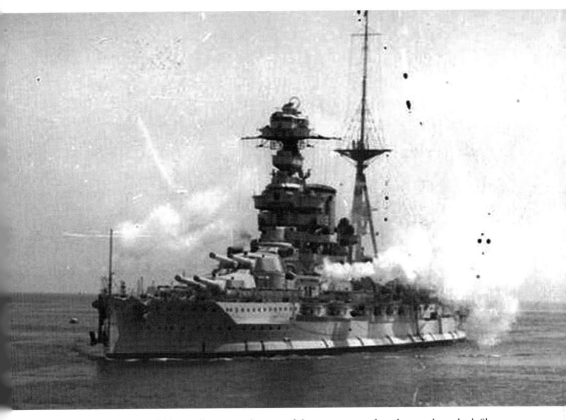

The battleship *Barham*, old but still immensely powerful, many years after she was launched. She is shown here firing her secondary armament in a pre-war practice shoot.

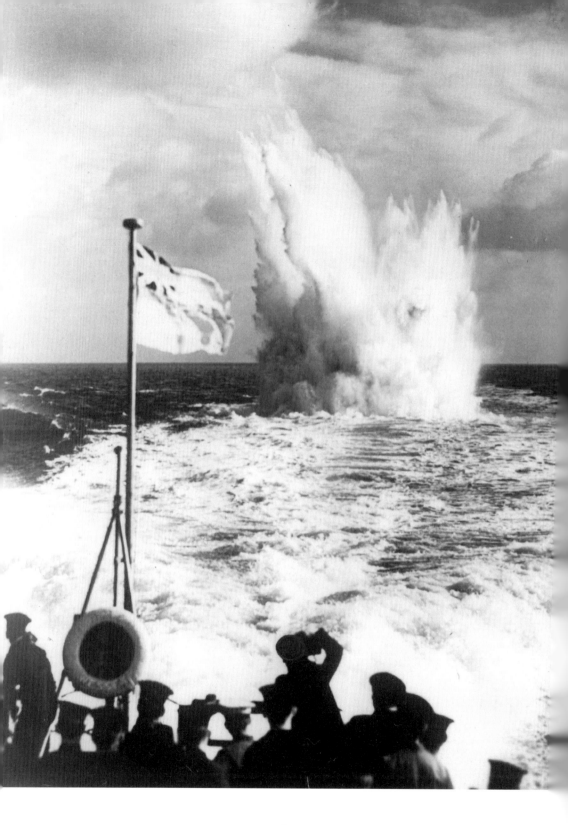

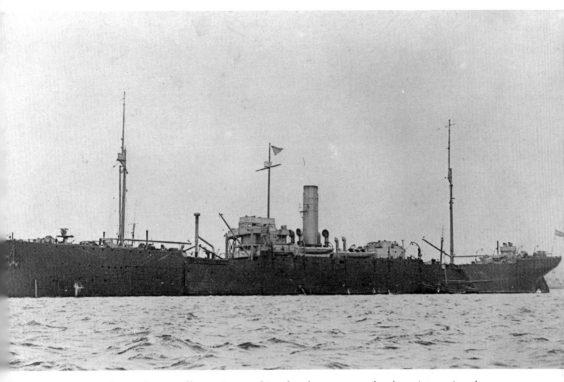

The destroyer depot ship *Sandhurst*. Depot ships for destroyers and submarines enjoyed an unglamorous war, but they player a crucially important role in keeping ships well armed and effective.

Opposite page: Depth charges exploding, seen from the stern of an attacking destroyer.

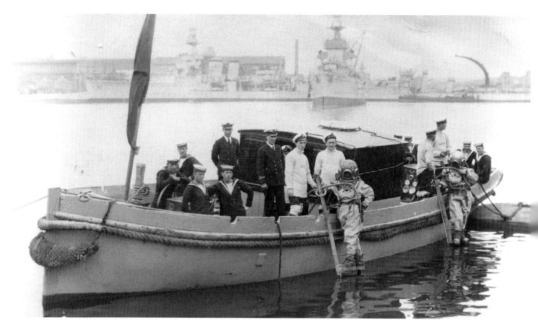

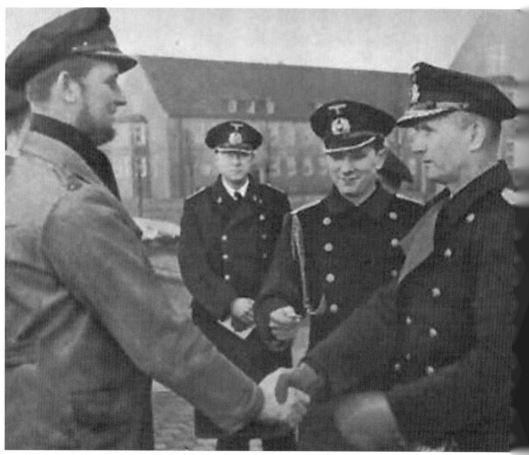

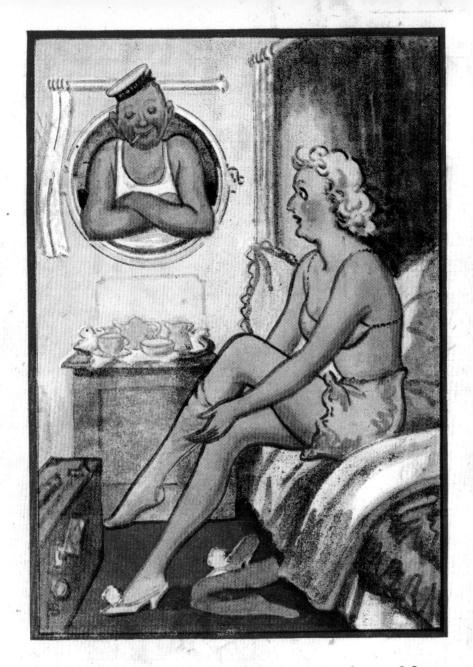

"Don't trouble to dress any further, Mum perhaps I didn't see a U-Boat after all!"

This comic postcard from the war years shows that the British never lost their sense of humour, regardless of how badly things were going at the front or on the sea. There were times when laughing at adversity seemed to be all anyone could do.

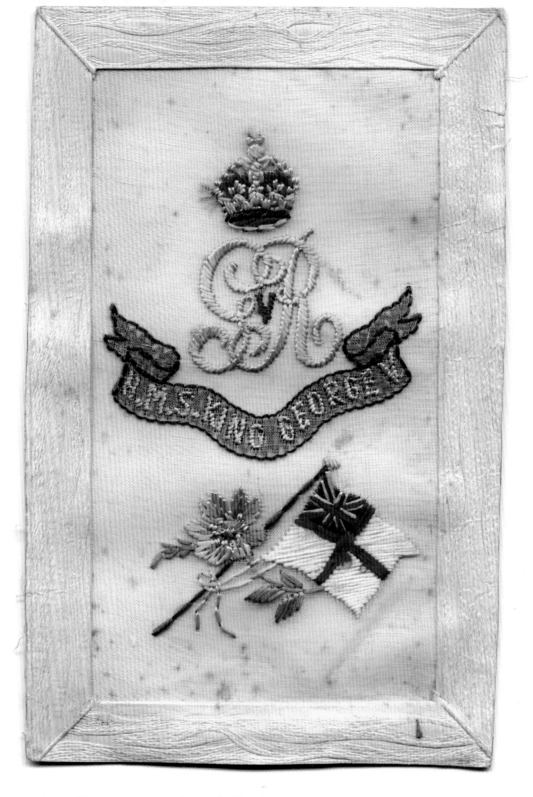

A rare silk postcard from the battleship *King George V*.

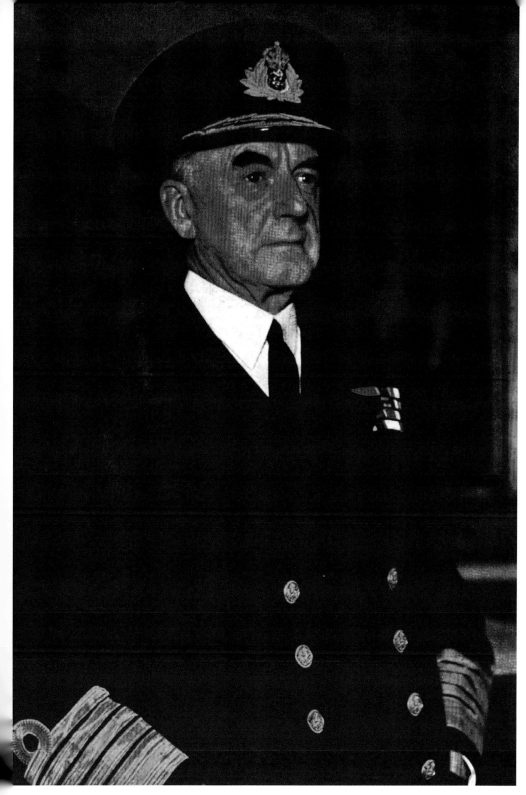

Sir Dudley Pound GCB, Admiral of the Fleet from July 1939 until his death in October 1943.

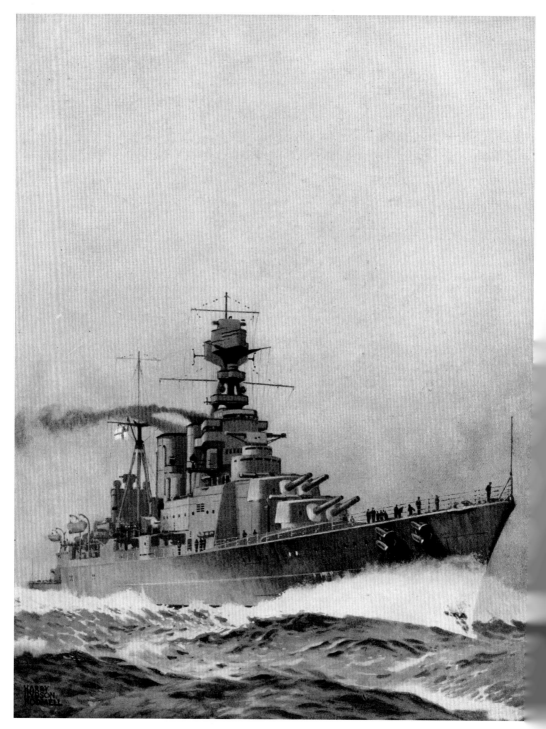

HMS *Hood*, the pride of the Royal Navy. She was the one ship that everybody knew – and loved.

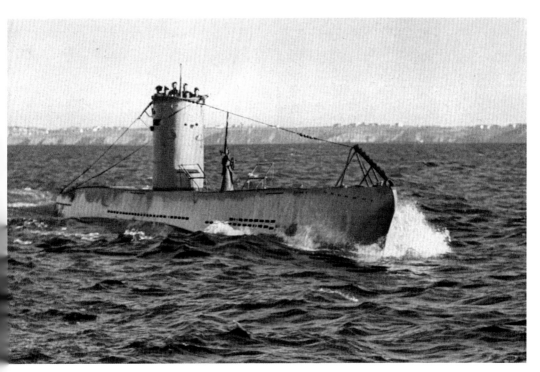

A German U-boat setting out on patrol.

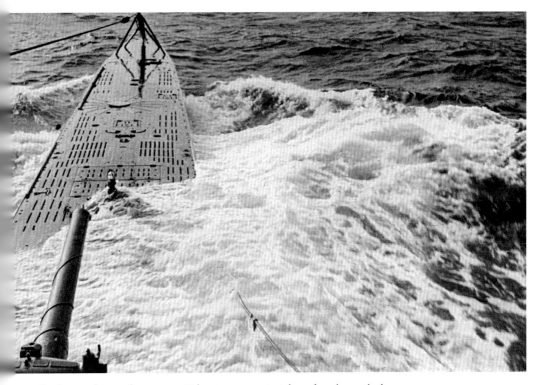

Getting ready to submerge – a U-boat prepares to take refuge beneath the waves.

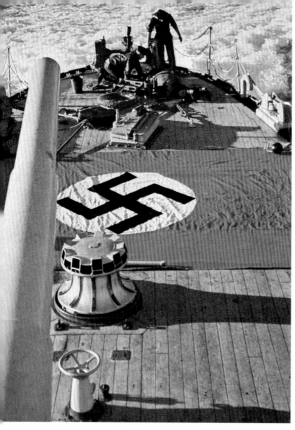

The Nazi flag is clearly visible in this view of the stern of a German cruiser.

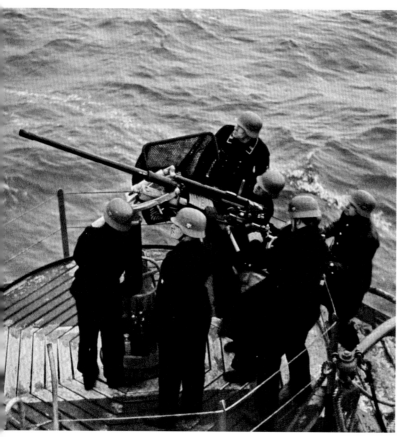

Anti-aircraft gunners on a German destroyer get ready to fire at British aeroplanes.

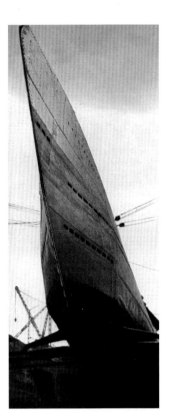

A submarine docked for repairs before heading out on patrol once more.

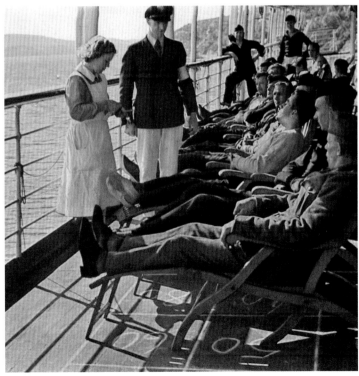

A German Kraft durch Freude ship, where people could relax for a brief period.

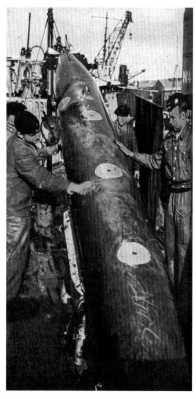

Preparing a torpedo for use by a German a U-boat.

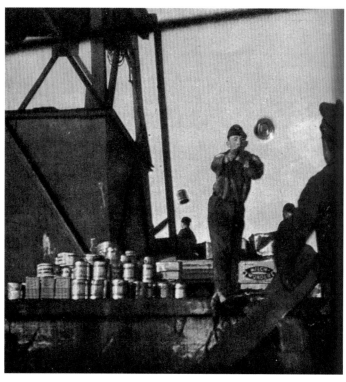

Resupplying a U-boat before it goes back on duty.

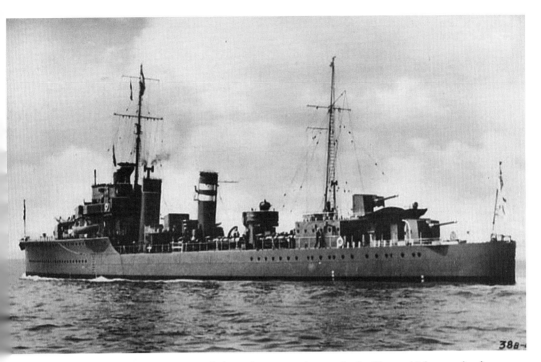

The flotilla leader *Faulkner*, one of three destroyers that sank the U39, which was the first German submarine loss of the war.

Opposite top: Divers at Chatham in their weighty and unwieldy gear. Divers were vital to the safety of the Royal Navy ships in dockyards like Chatham, but their role went largely unacknowledged.

Opposite bottom: Karl Dönitz, head of the German U-boat arm, congratulates one of his commanders. Dönitz was to lose two of his sons in the war, and finished it as supreme commander of the dying German empire after Hitler's suicide.

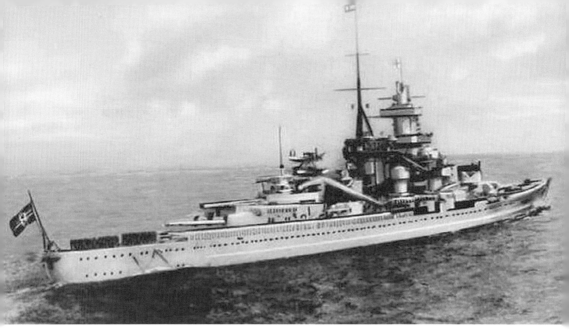

The battlecruiser *Gneisenau*, seen here from the stern.

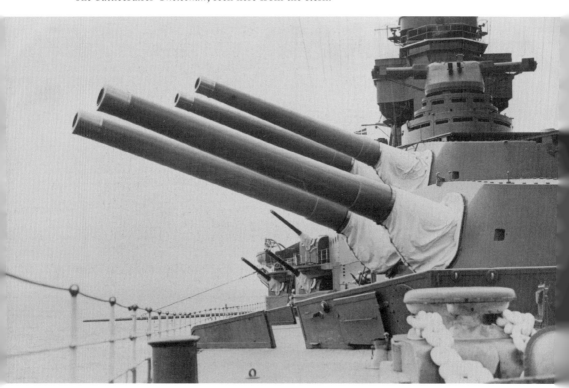

The mighty guns of HMS *Hood*. Like all battlecruisers, the *Hood* was well armed but too lightly armoured and so vulnerable to high, plunging shot – as the Admiralty later found out to their cost.

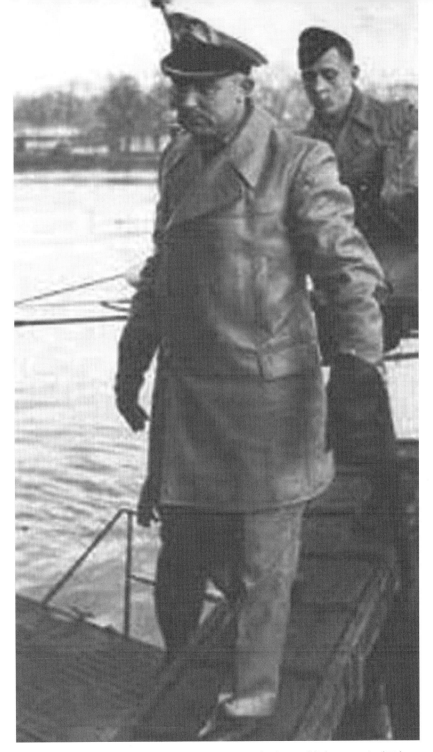

Günther Prien on the deck of his U-boat. Prien was the first publicly recognised U-boat ace of the war and, for a brief while, enjoyed celebrity status in Germany. He was later to die on his submarine but, while it lasted, Prien and his crew enjoyed their moment of glory.

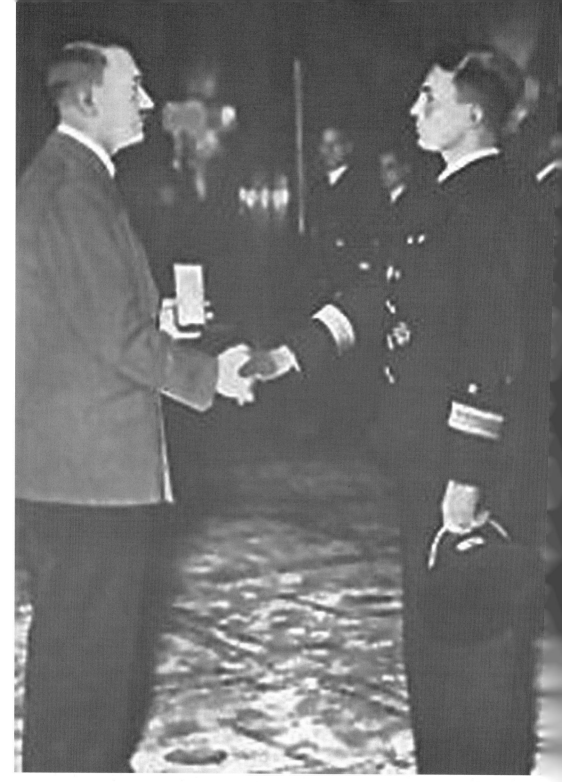

Adolf Hitler awards Prien the Knight's Cross after his successful attack on the *Royal Oak* in Scapa Flow.

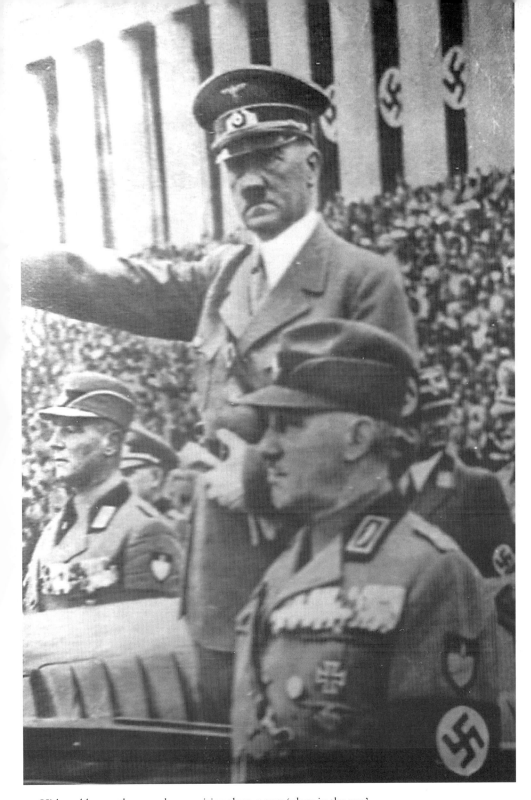

Hitler addresses the crowds, promising them a new 'place in the sun'.

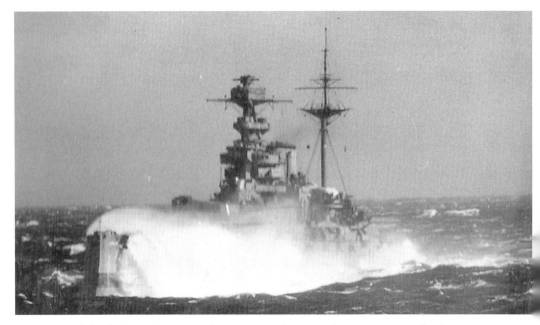

A British battleship in heavy seas, shipping tons of spray and green water over her bows.

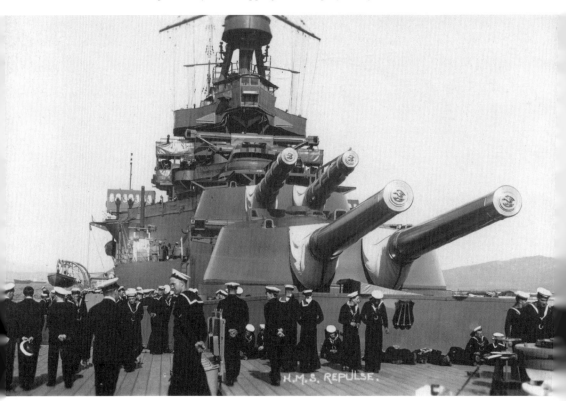

The guns and crew of the new *Repulse*, one of Britain's newest big gun vessels.

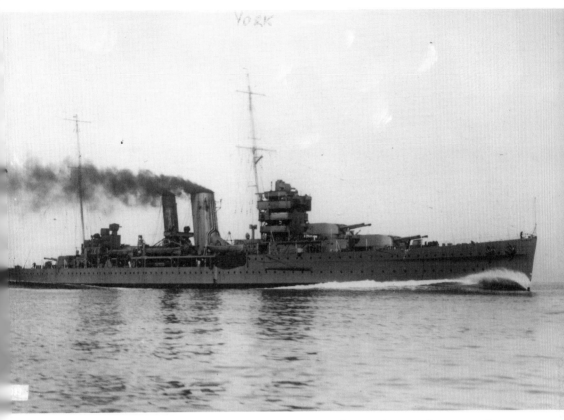

HMS *York*, a typical British cruiser of the 1930s, keeping within the treaty limits and, consequently, being under-gunned when it came to facing German and Japanese vessels of the same class.

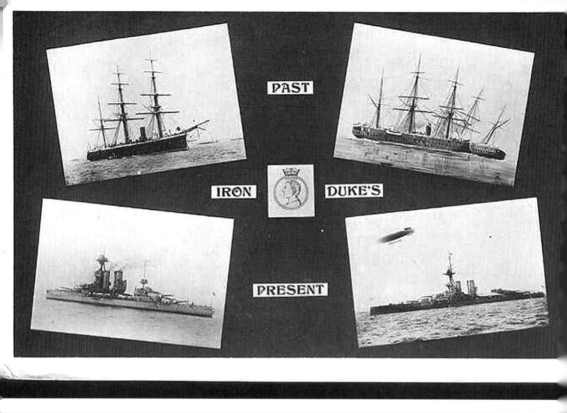

PAST

IRON DUKE'S

PRESENT

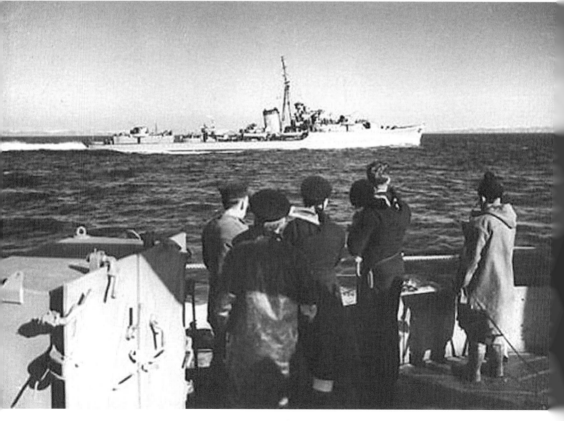

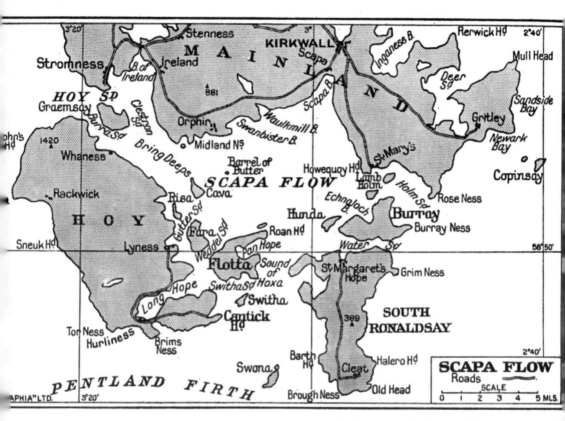

A map showing the location of Scapa Flow, the anchorage which, surrounded by the Orkney Islands, was the base of the British Home Fleet.

Opposite top: A composite postcard showing four different 'Iron Dukes'.

Opposite bottom: The destroyer *Kelly*, later the command of Lord Mountbatten. She had an active war, being damaged several times. Her exploits were immortalised in the film *In Which We Serve.*

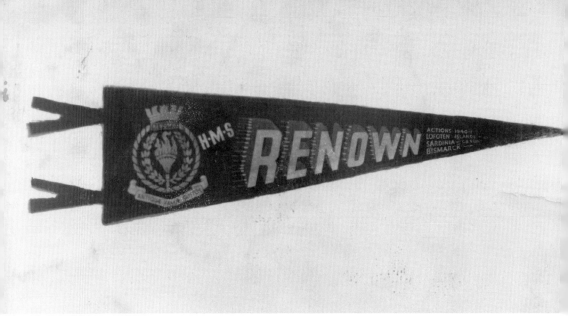

A pennant from the battleship *Renown*.

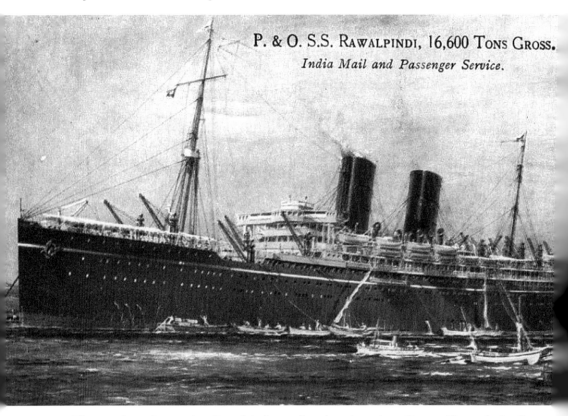

P. & O. S.S. RAWALPINDI, 16,600 TONS GROSS.
India Mail and Passenger Service.

The armed merchant cruiser *Rawalpindi*, seen here in quieter days. Her sacrifice undoubtedly saved many lives when she took on the battlecruisers *Scharnhorst* and *Gneisenau* in November 1939.

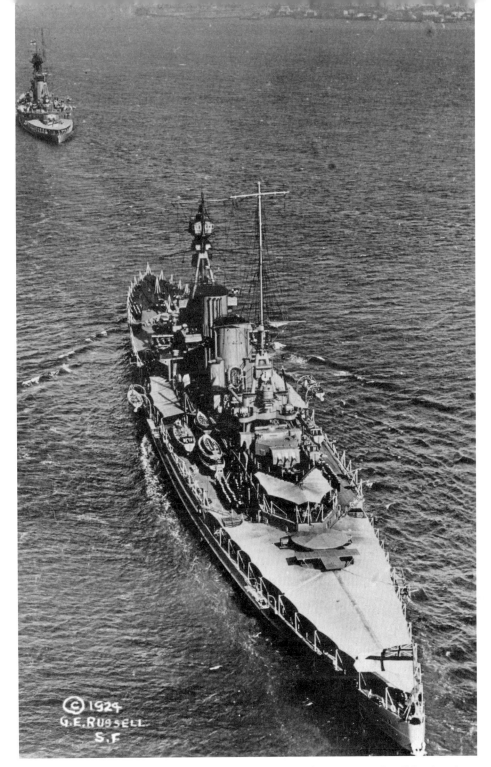

© 1924
G.E.RUSSELL
S.F

An aerial view of the *Renown*, one of the symbols of British seapower. Like all battlecruisers, however, weak deck armour made her vulnerable to aerial attack and plunging shot, and was a major defect in her design.

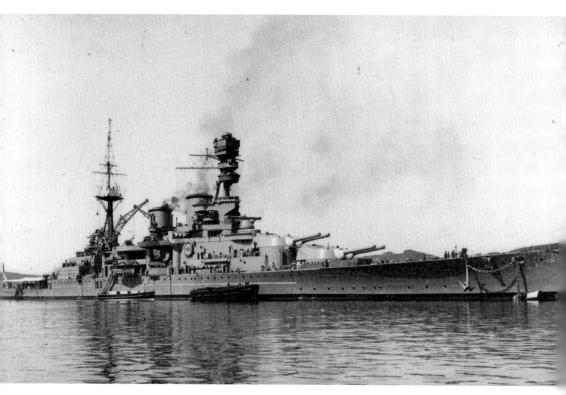

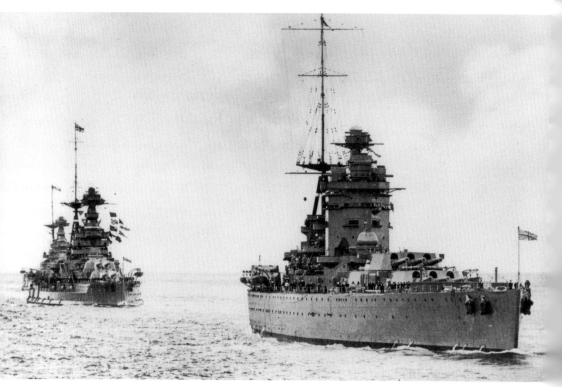

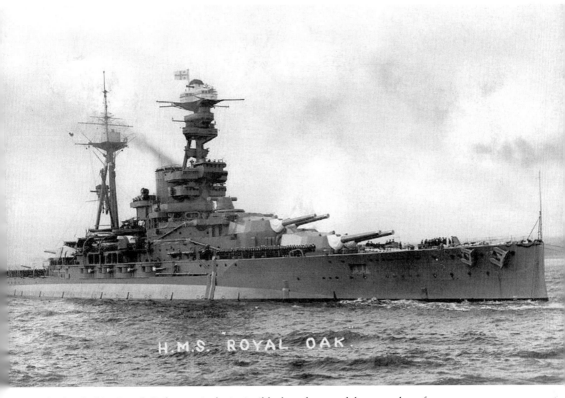

The battleship *Royal Oak*, seemingly invincible but destroyed by torpedoes from an unseen enemy in the opening weeks of the war.

Opposite top: The newly completed *Repulse*. Her guns provided a deterrent to any German surface raider she might encounter.

Opposite bottom: The *Rodney* and *Barham* at sea. Britain's battle fleet might have been old, but in 1939 it was still a powerful force that Hitler knew he would have to defeat.

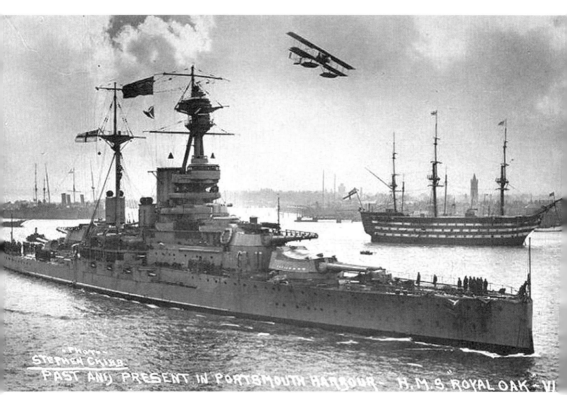

PAST AND PRESENT IN PORTSMOUTH HARBOUR · H.M.S. "ROYAL OAK" - VI

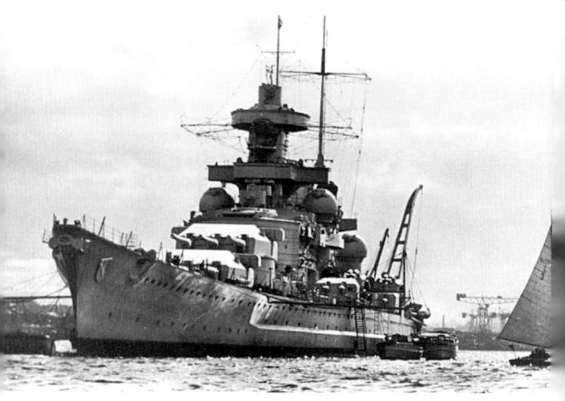

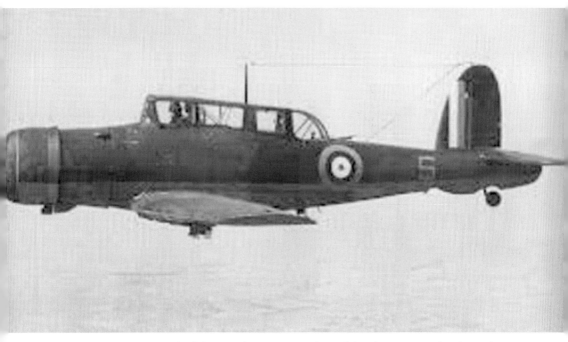

A Blackburn Skua. An aircraft of this type from 803 Squadron of the Fleet Air Arm shot down the first German aircraft of the war. However, by the end of 1939 the Skua was already approaching obsolescence. 803 Squadron was the first of two Fleet Air Arm squadrons, as the RFAA usually operated land- and carrier-based torpedo bombers.

Opposite top: The old and the new. The *Royal Oak* passes Nelson's flagship *Victory*, while a seaplane circles in the sky above. New technology in the shape of torpedoes would soon send the *Royal Oak* to the bottom.

Opposite bottom: The battlecruiser *Scharnhorst* is seen here at the dockside in Kiel. The raw power of the German battlecruiser is evident in this photograph.

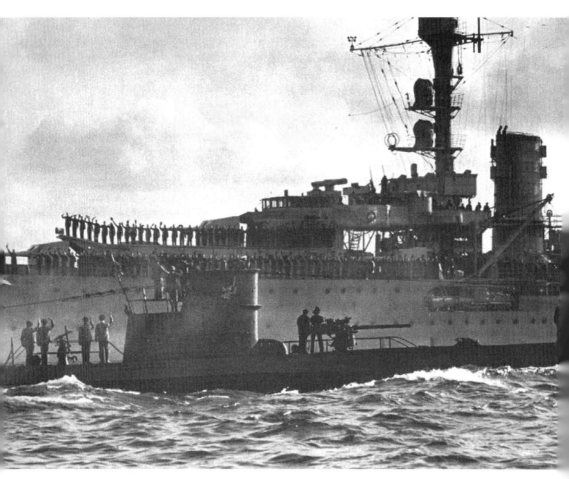

The U47 passes the cruiser *Emden* on her way out to another patrol. It is a classic portrayal of the old and the new – the *Emden* representing the old surface fleet, the U-boat encapsulating the new style of naval warfare, which would soon bring Britain to the brink of defeat for the second time in half a century.

Opposite page: The battleships *Warspite* and *Nelson*. This view is taken from the bridge of the *Nelson*, and shows the massive armament of the ship, and tiny paddle tugs in the space between the two battleships.

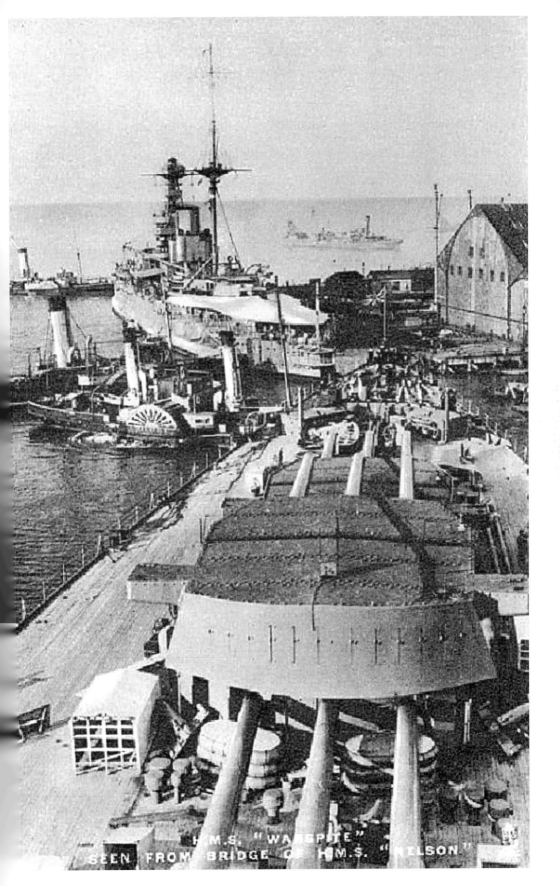

H.M.S. "WARSPITE"
SEEN FROM BRIDGE OF H.M.S. "NELSON"

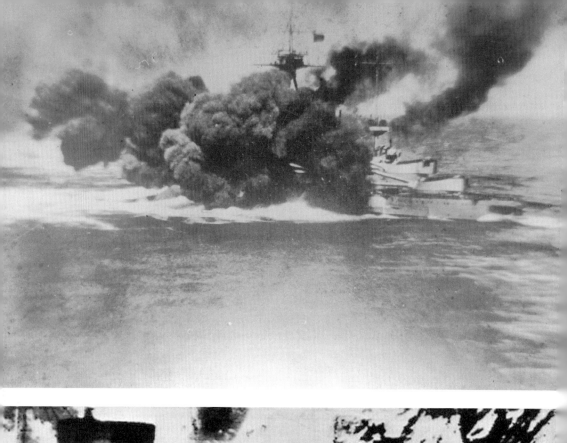
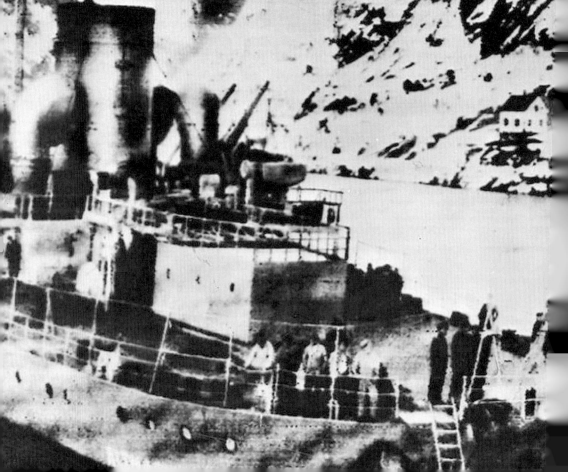

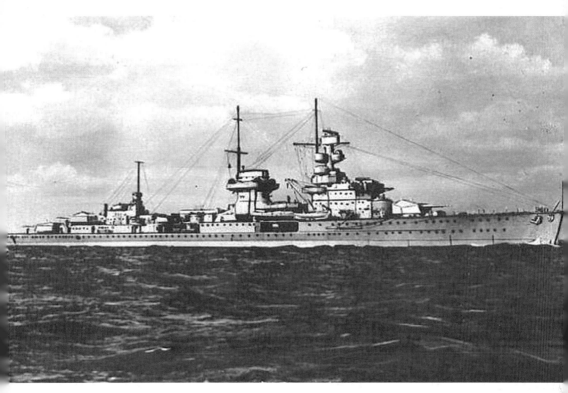

The light cruiser *Nürnberg*, one of several fast, well-armed vessels deployed by the Kriegsmarine in the early stages of the war. She carried a famous name – the original *Nürnberg*, another light cruiser, was lost during the Battle of the Falkland Islands in December 1914.

Opposite top: The guns of the *Warspite* open fire.

Opposite bottom: The supply ship *Altmark* operated in conjunction with the surface raider *Graf Spee*, and took those prisoners who could not be accommodated on the pocket battleship. This view shows the *Altmark* in the Norwegian fjord where, early in 1940, she was captured by the destroyer *Cossack*.

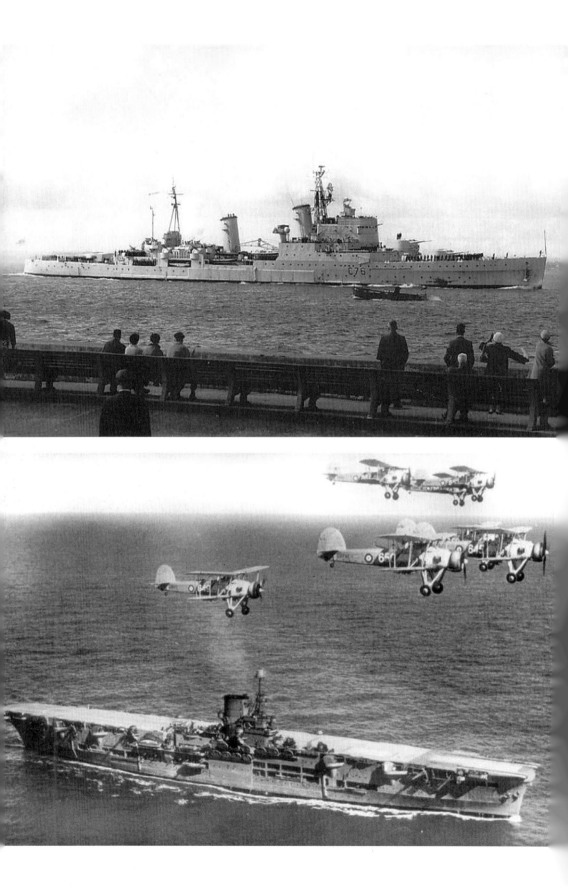

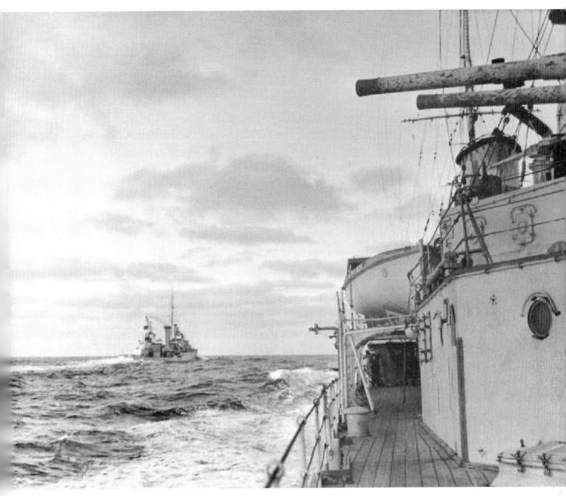

The *Achilles*, seen here from the deck of *Ajax* during the Battle of the River Plate. The *Achilles* was the only one of Commodore Harwood's small squadron not to sustain serious damage during the battle. Like *Ajax* and *Exeter*, she played her part in hounding the *Graf Spee* and, ultimately, in sending her to the bottom.

Opposite top: The cruiser *Newcastle*, which picked up survivors of the AMC *Rawalpindi* after she had been sunk by the *Scharnhorst* and *Gneisenau*.

Opposite bottom: This photograph shows the Swordfish torpedo bombers, ancient and already obsolete before the war began, of the carrier *Ark Royal*. The Swordfish were slow and cumbersome, which is possibly one of the reasons that anti-aircraft gunners on ships like the *Bismarck* failed to get their range and shoot them down.

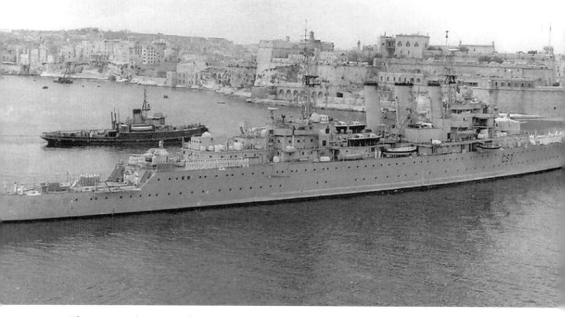

The missing ship – *Cumberland* was in the Falkland Islands for repairs when the Battle of the River Plate was fought. She rejoined Harwood's squadron once the *Graf Spee* was blockaded into Montevideo harbour.

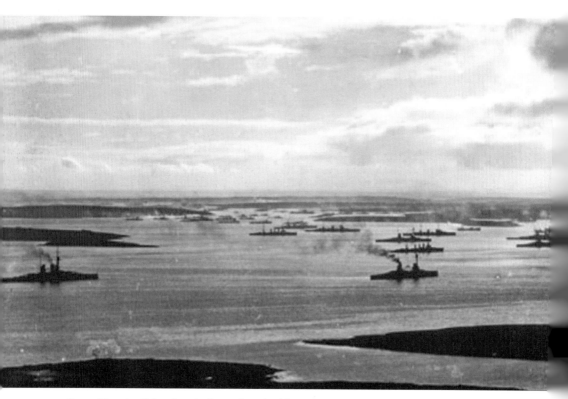

Scapa Flow in all its glory is shown here in this panoramic view.

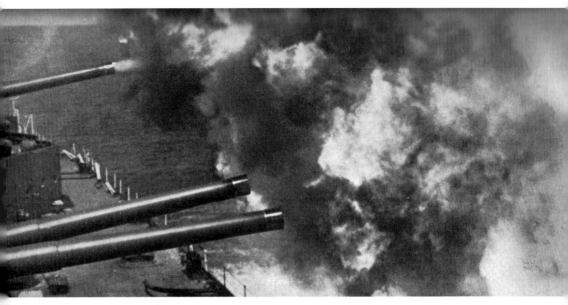

Shells being fired from the *Iron Duke*. By 1939, *Iron Duke* was in reserve, but her mighty 12-inch guns could still be useful.

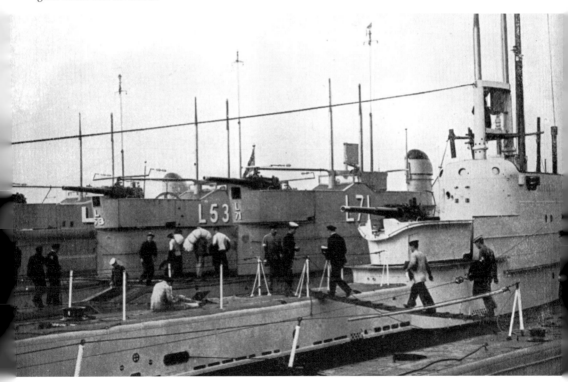

Submarine crew preparing to sail on another patrol. British and German sailors alike would have recognised the scene of hectic activity.

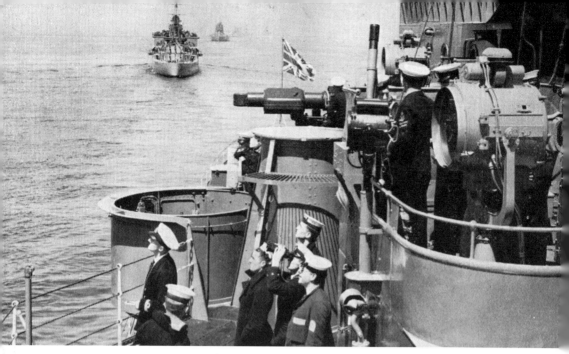

Sailors observing military manoeuvres aboard HMS *Glasgow*.

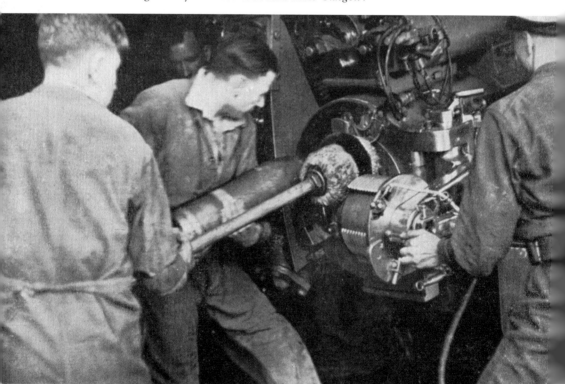

Gunnery officers and ratings training on HMS *Iron Duke* in Scapa Flow.

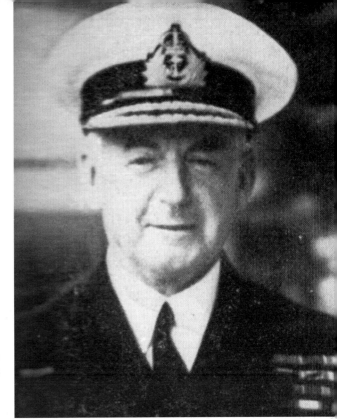

Admiral Sir Charles Morton Forbes, Commander-in-Chief of the Home Fleet from 1938 until December 1940. Forbes had fought with distinction in the First World War and was always a 'seagoing' admiral.

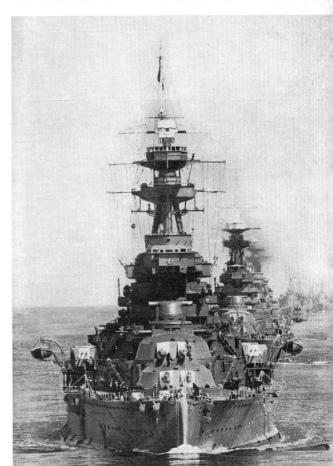

A view of British battleships in line astern, undoubtedly an awesome sight for friend or foe alike.

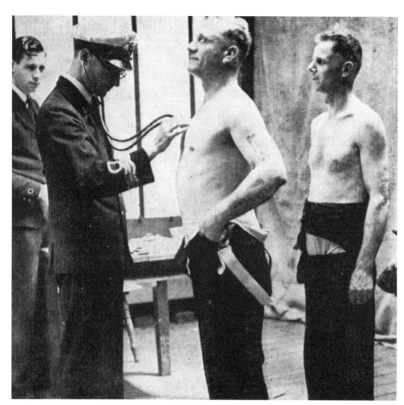

With the threat of war in the air, naval reservists were called back to the Colours in August 1939 and, as with all reservists or new conscripts, had to undergo an immediate physical examination.

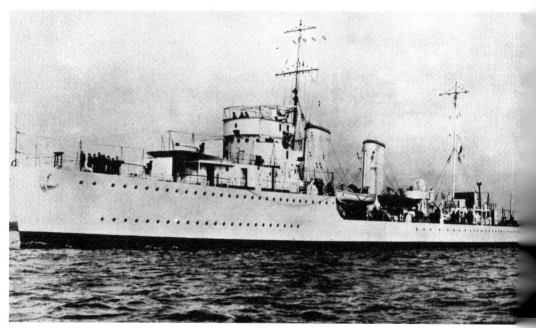

The destroyer *Sanguenay* of the Royal Canadian Navy. As in the First World War, the Dominions played an active role in the battle against Adolf Hitler. Ships from Canada, Australia and New Zealand were actively involved in all aspects of the conflict.

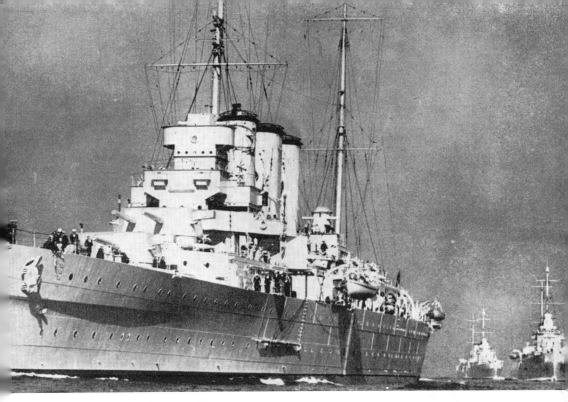

HMS *Canberra* of the Australian Navy.

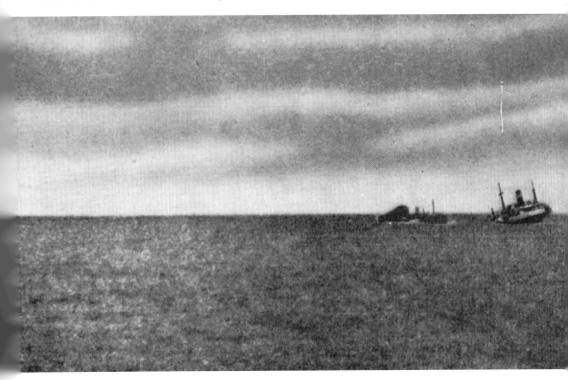

SS *Athenia* as she sank, having been hit by a torpedo.

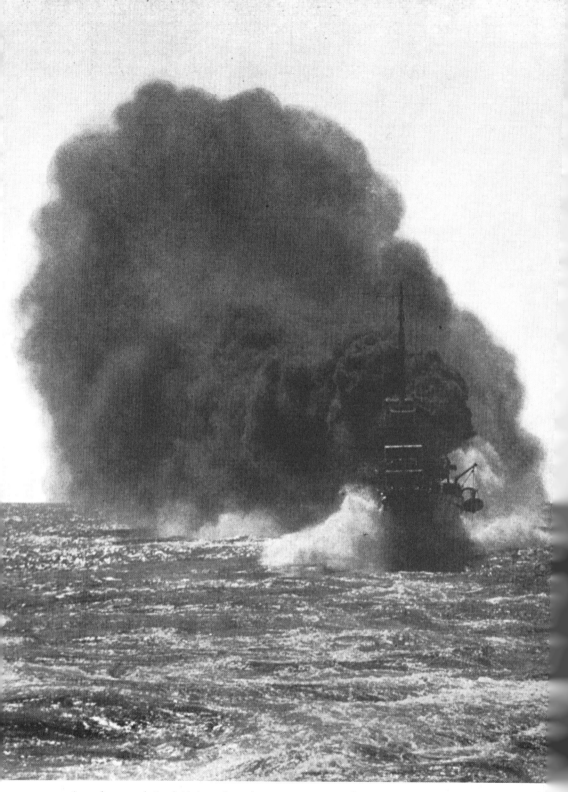

A smokescreen being laid down by a destroyer on convoy duties.

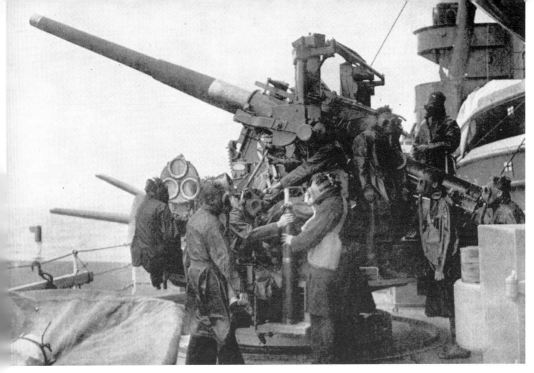

Above: Anti-aircraft guns aboard HMS *Nelson.*

Below: A Royal Navy destroyer involved in minesweeping is shown here, with a long, torpedo-like paravane being hoisted in to the water. It was a dangerous and often tedious occupation – until a mine was spotted. It was, however, a necessary job. The mine, like the torpedo, was a silent and brutal killer, and was merciless to merchant ships and warships alike.

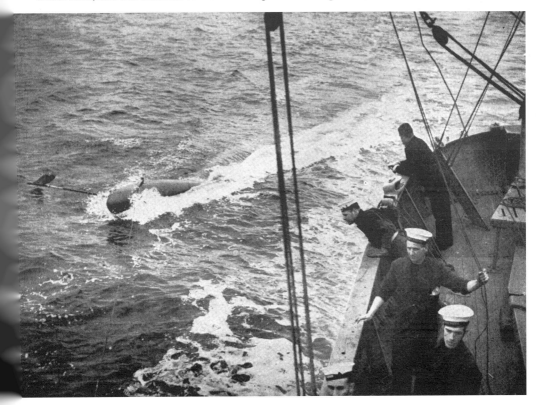

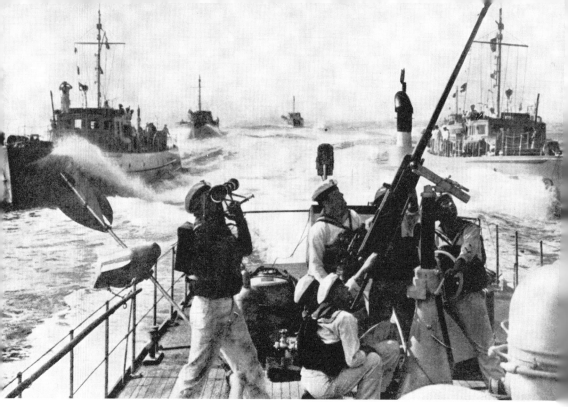

German sailors man their anti-aircraft guns on board minesweepers and E-boats off the coast of France.

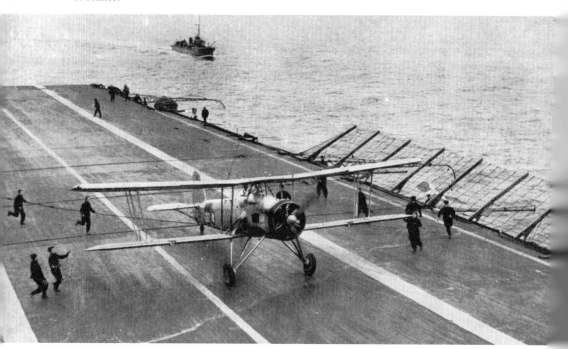

A Swordfish torpedo bomber about to take off from the deck of HMS *Courageous*.

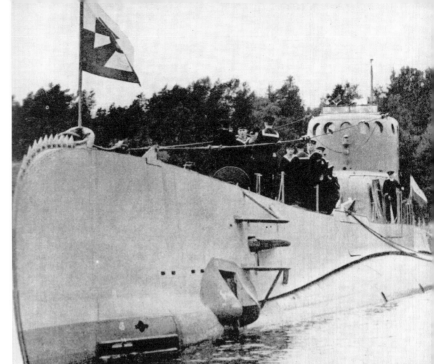

A Polish submarine interned in Sweden after fleeing her home waters following the defeat of Poland in 1939.

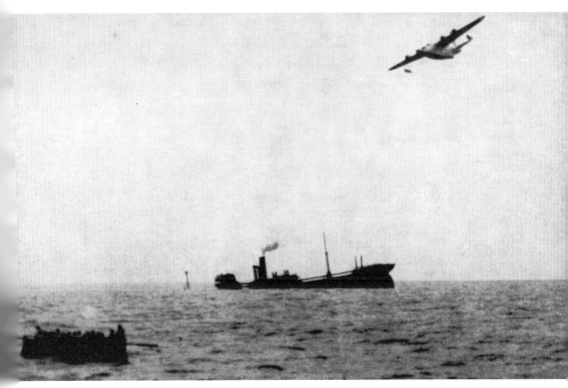

The crew of a doomed merchant ship are rescued by aircraft from the RAF Coastal Command. The sailors sit forlornly in their lifeboat as their ship sinks slowly by the bows. Their one consolation is that they will not have to spend days adrift in their open boats.

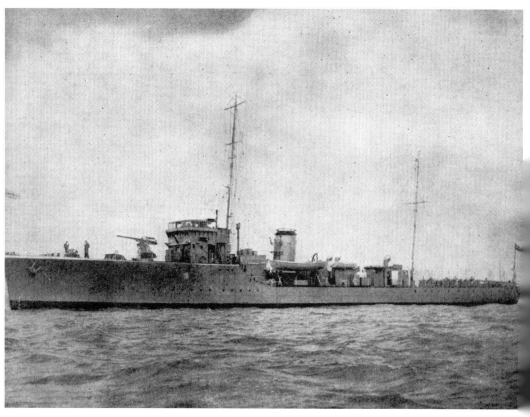

The sloop *Kittiwake*, which was struck by a bomb in the early days of the war.

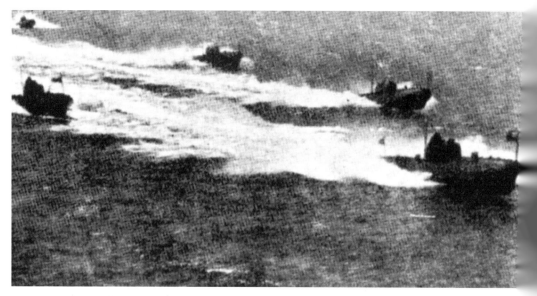

Russian torpedo boats, small inshore craft that had a short range but were highly effective against slower merchant vessels and warships. In 1939, Russia was an ally of Germany, engaged in attacking Finland and helping to dismember the remains of conquered Poland.

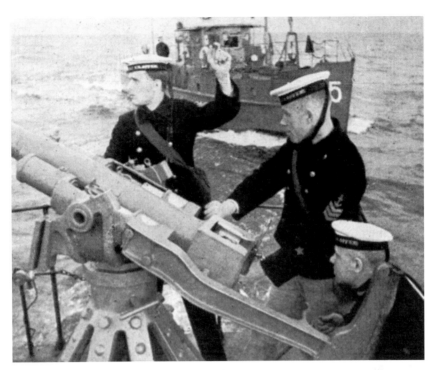

Machine-gun practice on board a Russian ship.

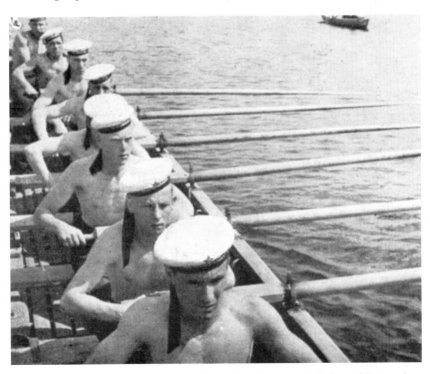

Rowing practice for navy recruits. It might not have been particularly useful in modern warfare but rowing certainly helped to keep sailors fit.

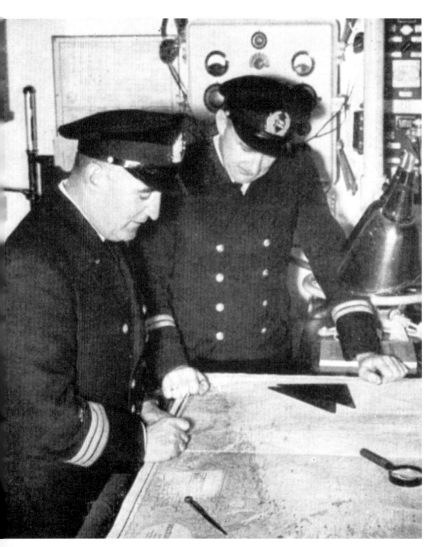

Naval officers study their charts, trying to understand German minelaying activity.

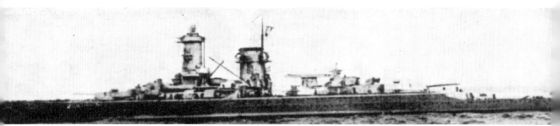

The *Admiral Scheer*, which, like German capital ships, caused more than a few headaches for British naval planners in the early days of the war. As it turned out, the *Scheer* was always something of an empty threat.

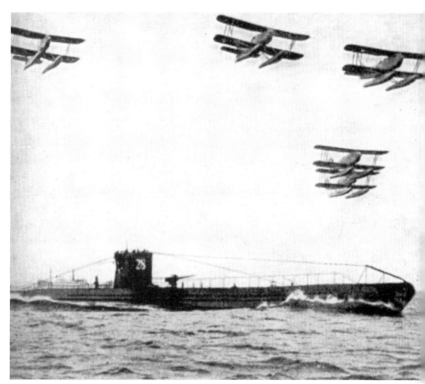

The U28, with seaplanes flying above, a pre-war shot intended for publicity purposes.

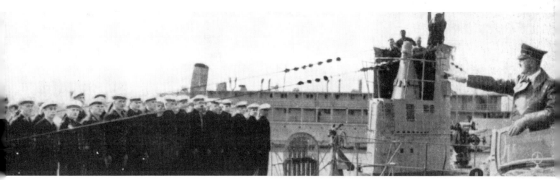

Adolf Hitler gives a motivational address to the crew of a German U-boat. As the war progressed and the U-boats entered what their crew called 'the happy time', the submariners needed little motivation; their successes were enough.

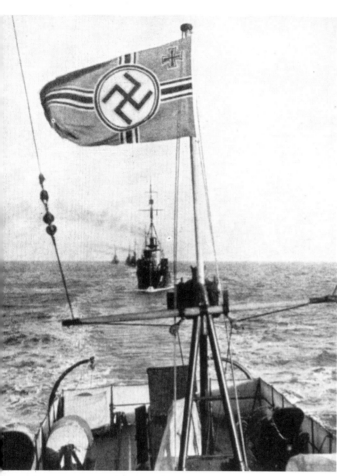

German minesweepers flying the
Nazi flag.

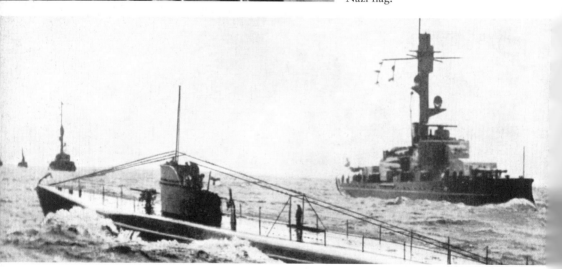

Finnish naval ships during the campaign against Russia in 1939.

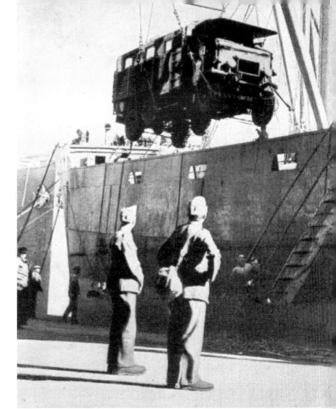

Right: A transport ship delivering vehicles to France.

Below: An officer scales the side of a merchant ship, coming on board to look for contraband. Stopping neutral vessels and searching for armaments or other contraband were necessary evils, but caused considerable offence to neutral countries like Sweden and the USA.

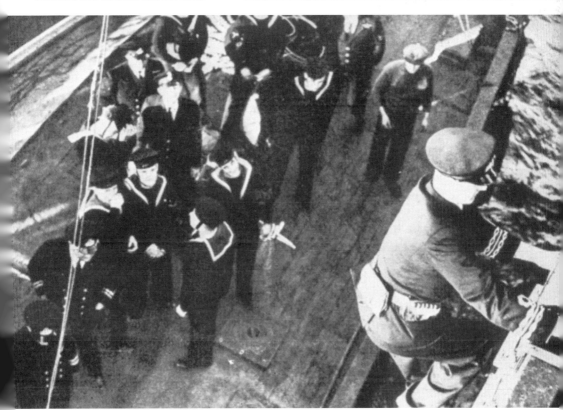

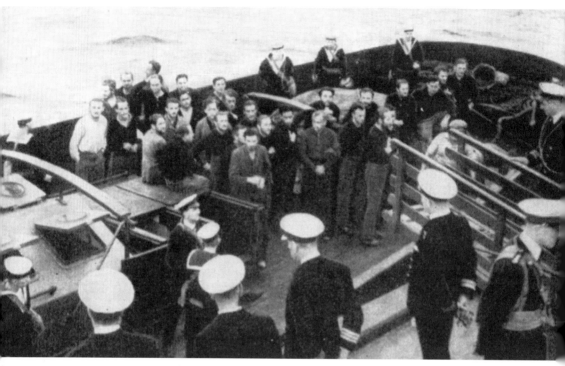

A captured U-boat crew about to be interned.

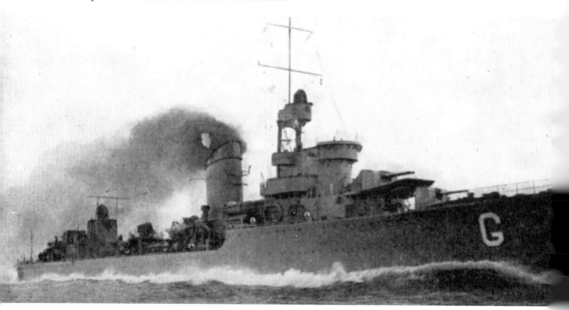

Above: A Polish destroyer. Within six weeks of war being declared, Poland was beaten, and her navy played virtually no further part in the conflict.

Opposite page: British anti-aircraft gunners taking a shot during one of the routine convoy trips across the Atlantic.

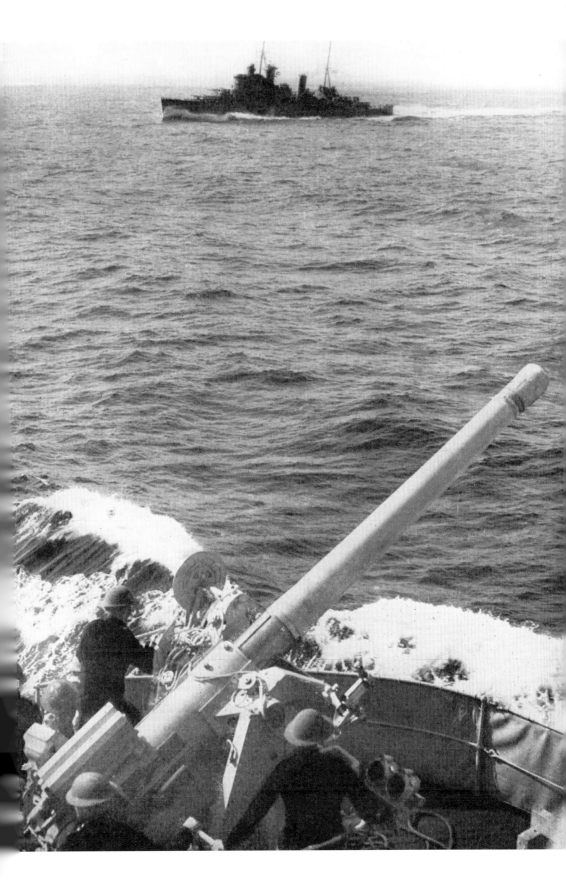

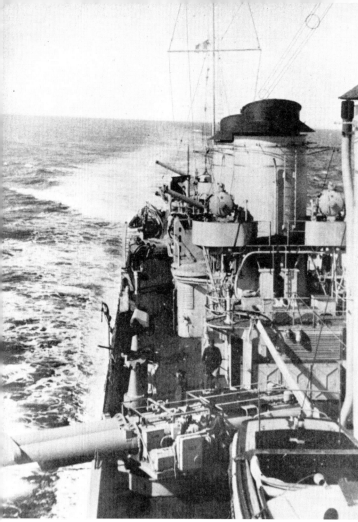

A French destroyer about to launch a torpedo. The combination of the British and French navies seemed to be a strong one, but with the defeat of France in 1940, Britain was denied the support of her ally's strong naval presence, particularly in the Mediterannean.

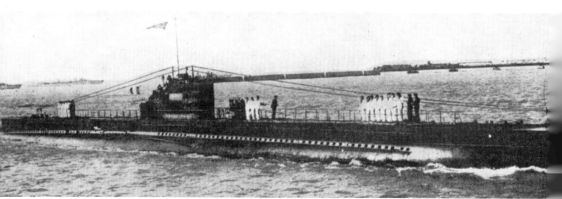

A French submarine, complete with crew assembled on the foredeck.

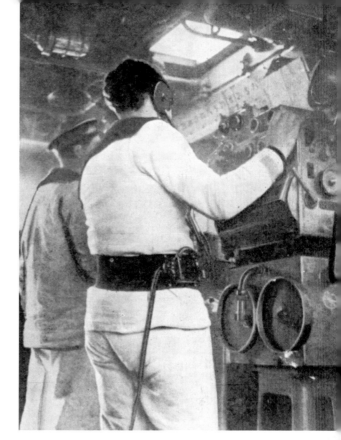

The gun control room on a French warship.

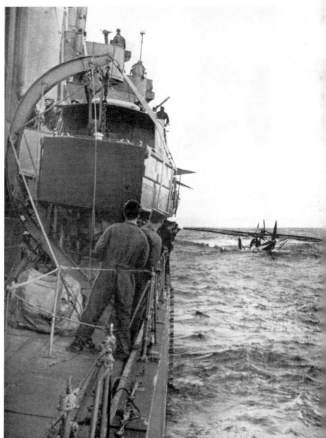

British sailors rescuing the crew of a German raider.

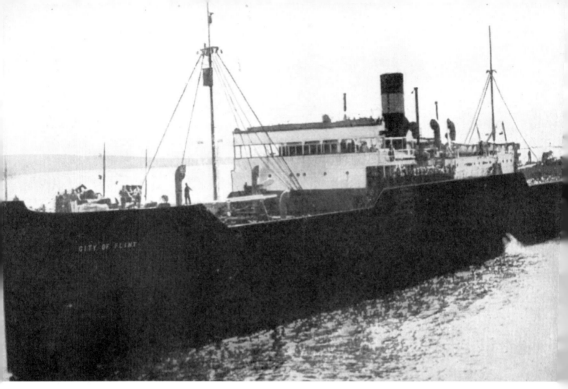

American ship *City of Flint*, which was captured by the Germans in 1939.

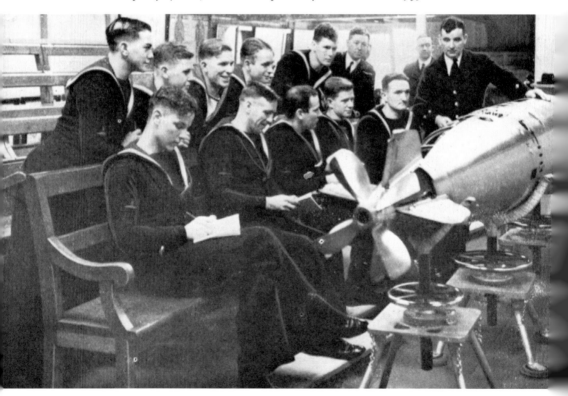

Learning their trade! British naval recruits are taught all about the deadly torpedoes.

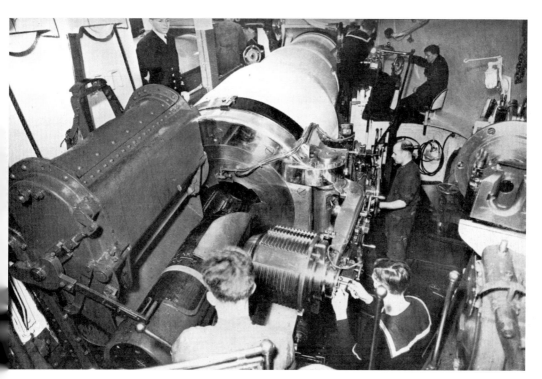

A turret gun on HMS *Iron Duke*.

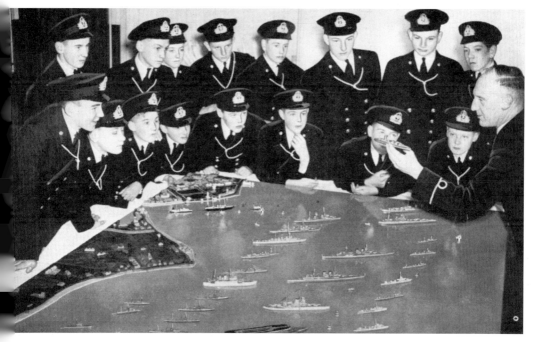

Naval officer training, using accurate and realistic scale models to depict fleet dispositions and movements.

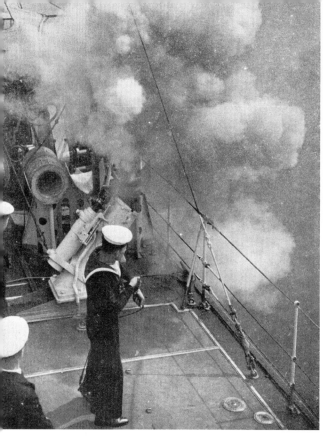

Ratings on a British destroyer using a depth charge thrower.

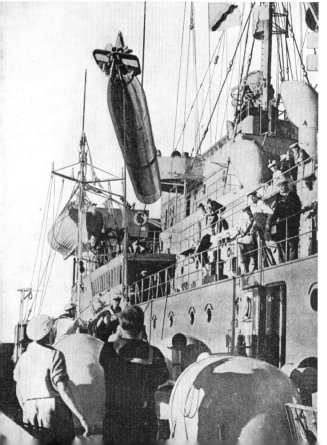

A German destroyer in the process of rearming herself with new torpedoes.

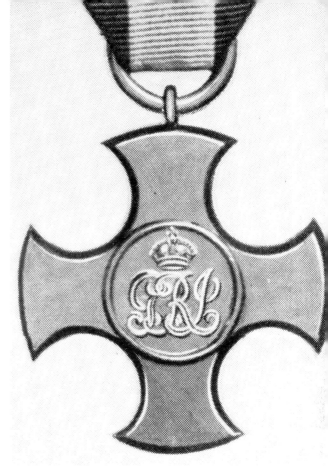

Right: The Distinguished Service Cross, the medal awarded to naval officers.

Below: Inside a hospital ship. Most large vessels had their own sick bay, but more serious cases were accommodated on ships like this.

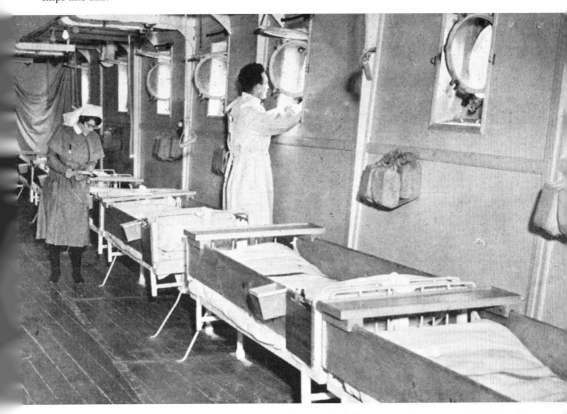

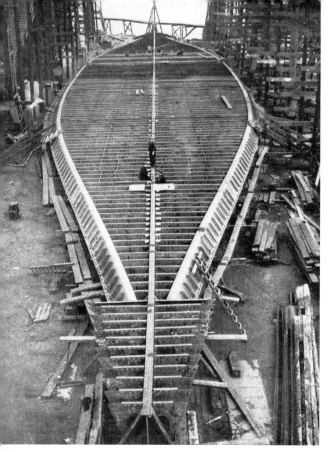

Left: A new ship being built for the Navy. Building new and replacement vessels, warships and merchantmen alike, was vital for the war effort, and continued until 1945.

Below: One of the many victims of German mines, the *Simon Bolivar*, which was sunk with the loss of eighty-three lives in the first few months of the war.

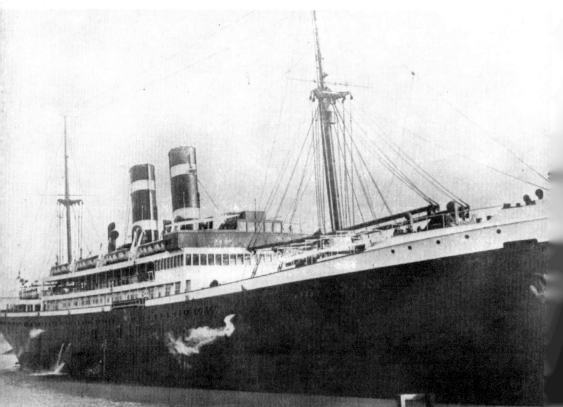

Lifeboat drills were important for anyone taking to the sea during the war years. Practices like this may have been useful, but doing it for real, at night, with the roar of guns and explosions ringing in your ears, would have been a different matter altogether.

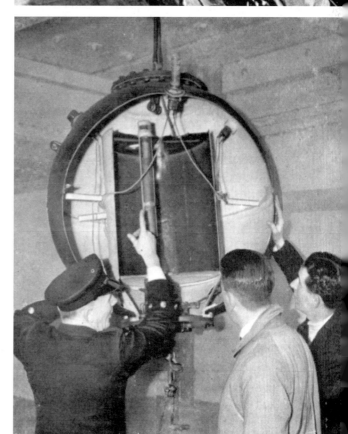

Merchant Navy sailors in the process of learning about mines – understanding the enemy's weapons was one way of keeping ships and personnel safe.

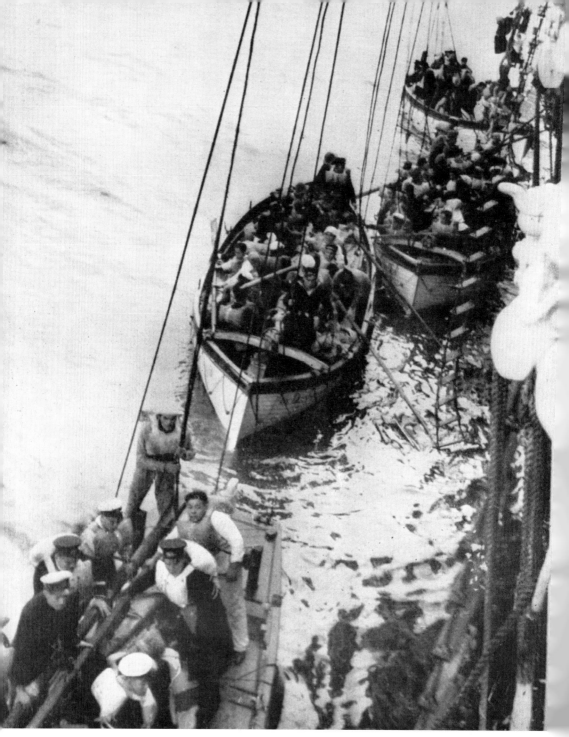

Victims from a ship that hit a German mine are seen here being rescued from their lifeboats. Sometimes sailors could spend days adrift in their boats and rescue was often a matte of pure luck. Not all ships carried radio, and often they went to the bottom before anybody in the outside world knew anything about it. If another vessel happened to come along, the passengers and crew would be saved; if not, they could all die of thirst, starvation or hypothermia.

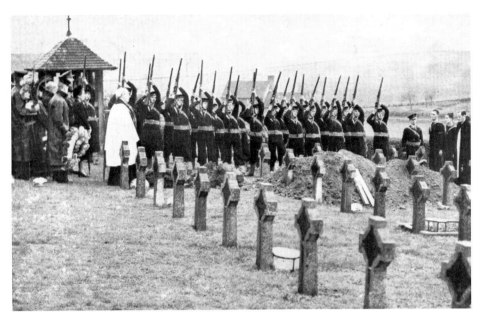

The burial of the commander of the *Gipsy*, one of the many vessels mined and sunk in the early days of the war.

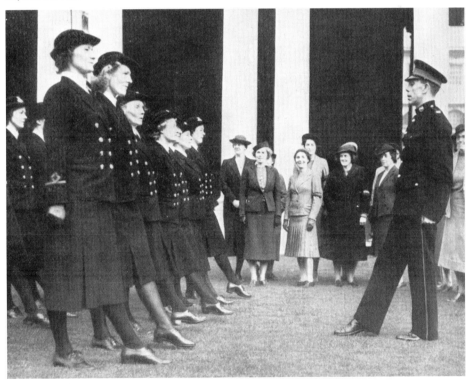

New members of the Women's Royal Naval Service learning how to march. The WRNS were re-formed in 1939, having been disbanded at the end of the First World War, and went on to perform heroically throughout the new conflict.

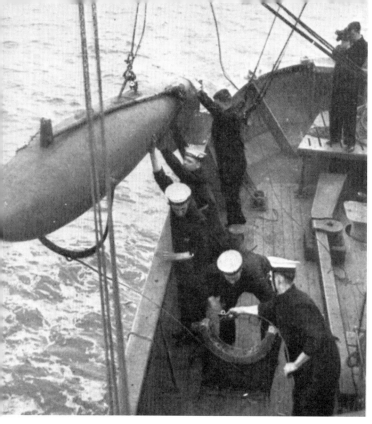

Left: In this photograph, a paravane is being floated in to the water alongside this British minesweeper.

Below: The German *Chemnitz,* which was captured by a French submarine.

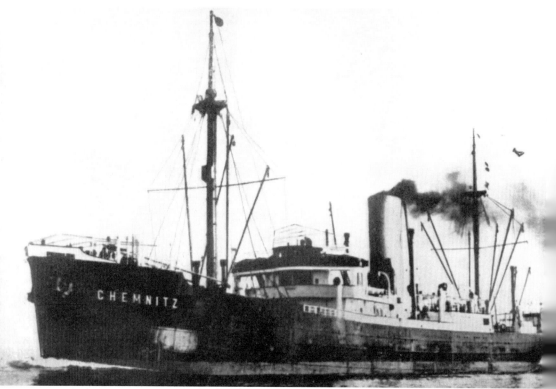

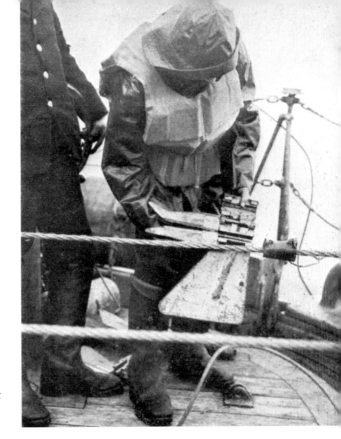

It might look basic, but this instrument was regularly used to cut the cables of floating mines.

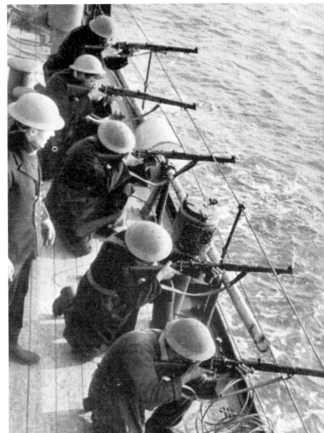

Preparing to destroy a mine by rifle fire – not the easiest of tasks but regarded by some as 'good sport'.

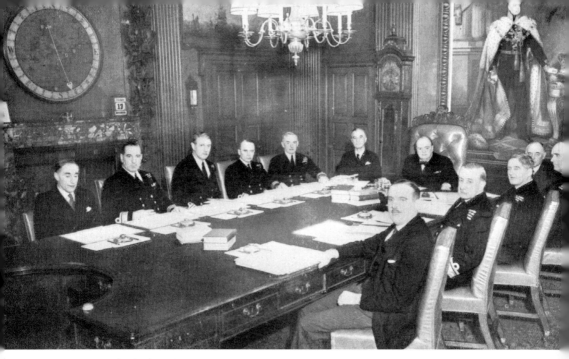

The Board of Admiralty in session.

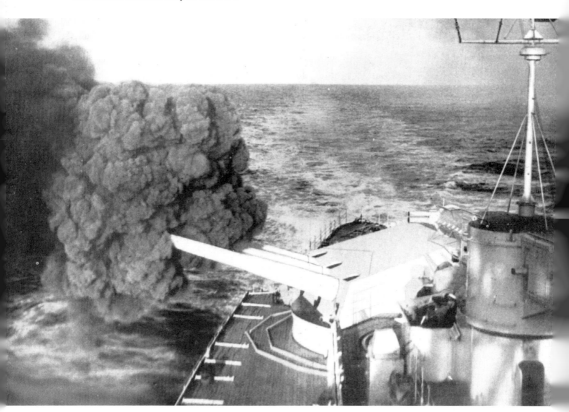

A German warship firing its guns. The dense smoke caused by firing would have been a major problem for spotters and range finders – something all sailors had to cope with.

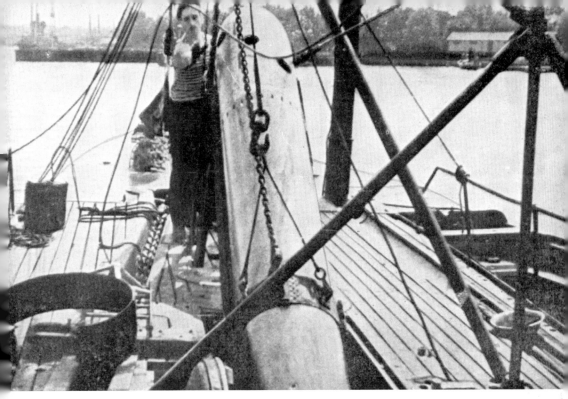

Loading a torpedo on to a French ship.

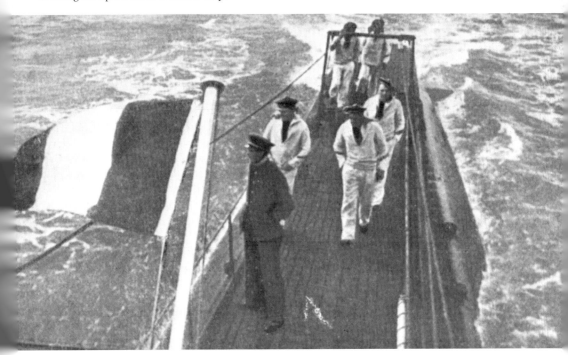

A French submarine crew enjoys the fresh air before going back down below deck. Conditions in the cramped hulls of submarines were basic in the extreme, and sailors were only too happy to take what opportunity they could to enjoy the wind and sea air.

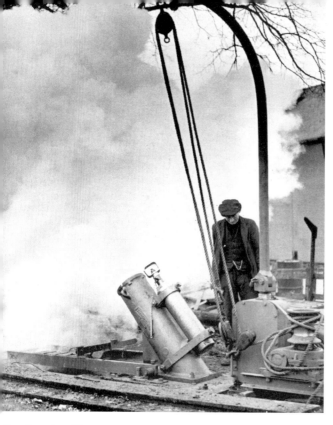

Depth charge testing at one of Britain's dockyards.

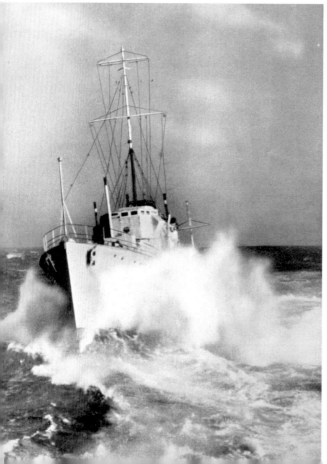

A submarine chaser in heavy seas.

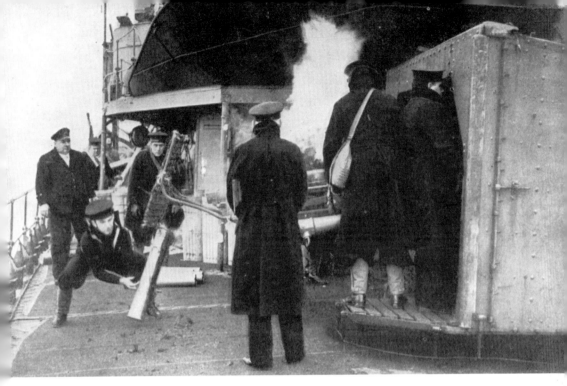

Gunnery training for British ratings.

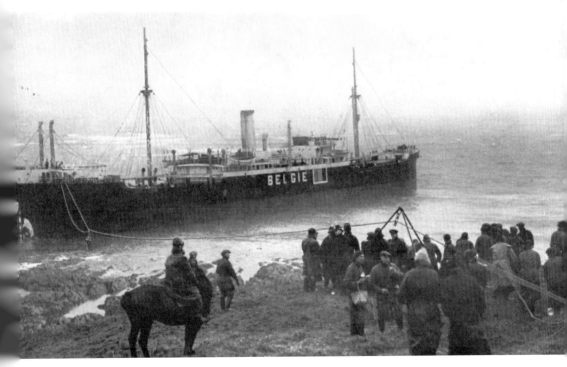

The Belgian rescue ship *Louis Scheid*.

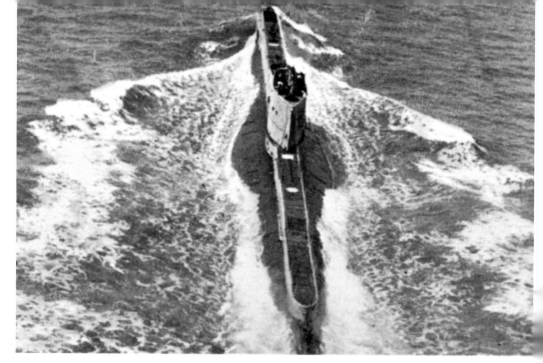

A submarine seen from the air. The photograph shows, quite clearly, how tiny the submarines were. Locating and spotting them from several thousand feet up in the air was never an easy task – never mind destroying them.

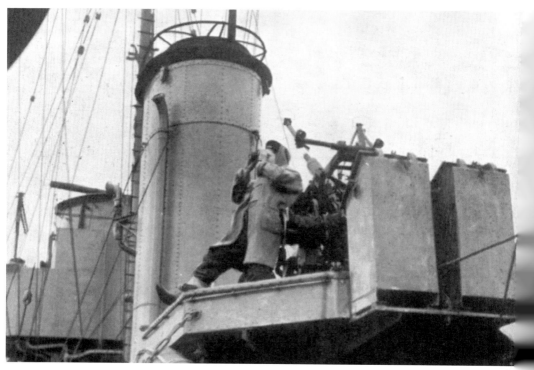

Sailors on a destroyer keeping watch for German aircraft. It was all too easy to be surprised by a sudden attack from the air.

Right: Battleships on patrol in the North Sea and along the Scandinavian coast.

Below: The king inspecting one of the Royal Navy destroyers. The royal family had always had strong connections with the Navy, and made regular visits to the fleet. During the war such visits were rarely ceremonial, but, in theory at least, part of a morale-boosting experience for the sailors.

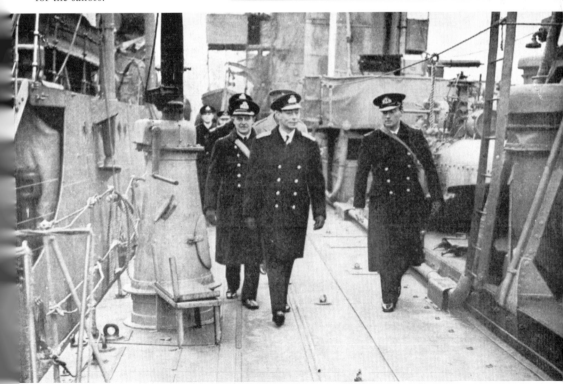

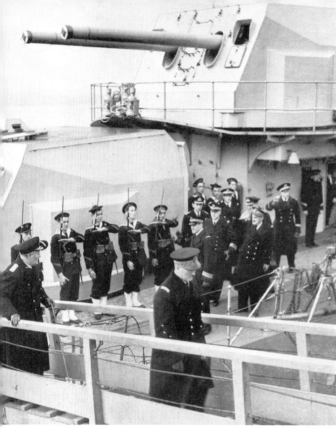

The Commander-in-Chief of the French navy visiting British ships.

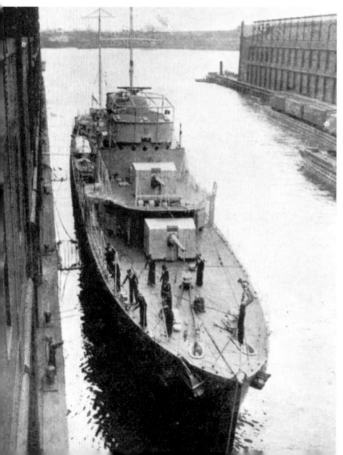

A Canadian destroyer in port after escorting a vital convoy across the Atlantic.

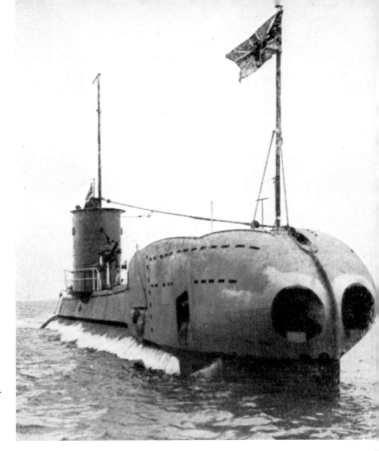

Right: The submarine *Ursula*, which destroyed a German cruiser.

Below: The demise of the *Admiral Graf Spee* in December 1939; this is the classic view of the sunken German commerce raider.

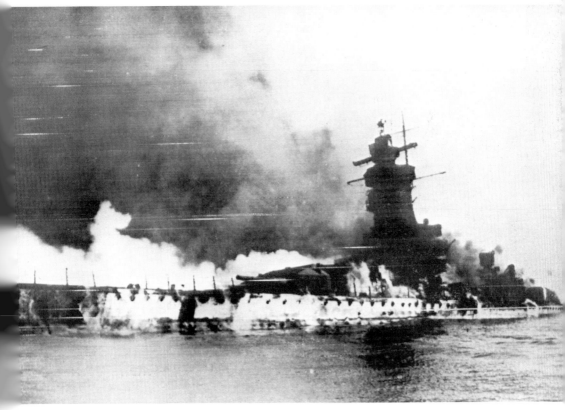

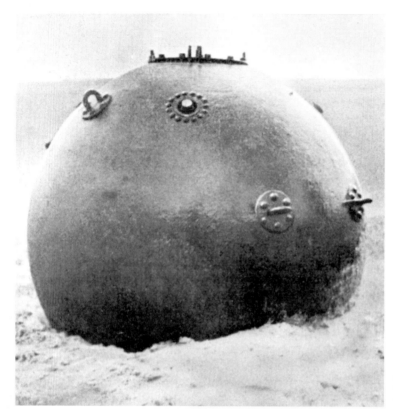

A German mine
washed up on the
beach in France.

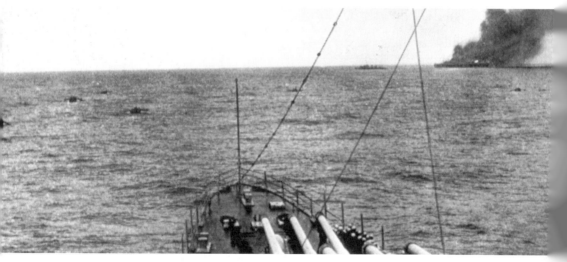

The end of the liner *Columbus*, one of the many merchant vessels destroyed during the conflict.

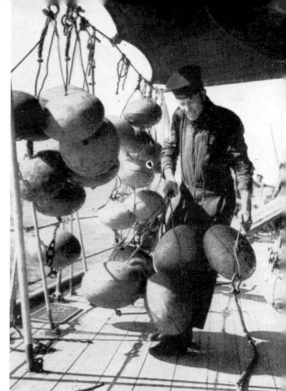

Right: Buoys were used to indicate which channels had been swept for mines and, therefore, which was the safe way in and out of port.

Below: British minesweepers at work in the North Sea.

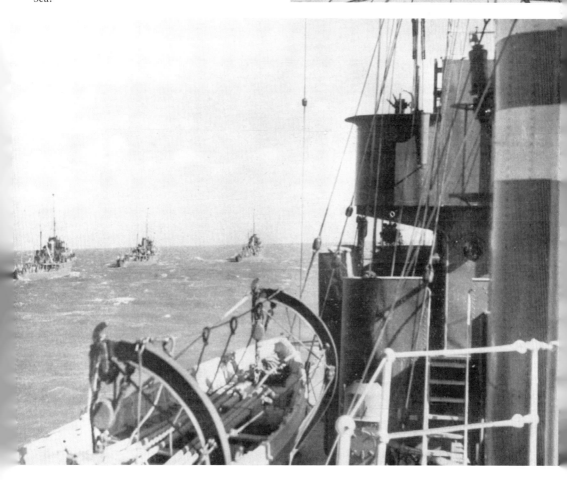

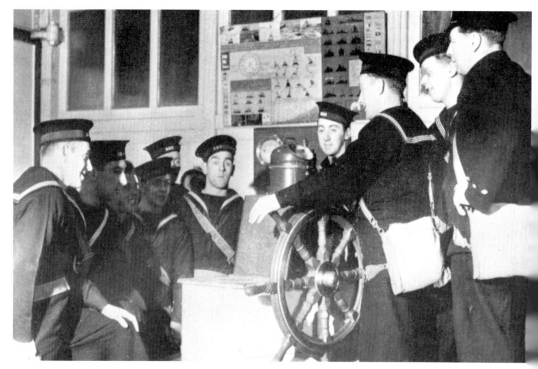

Training for ratings in the delicate but essential art of steering a ship.

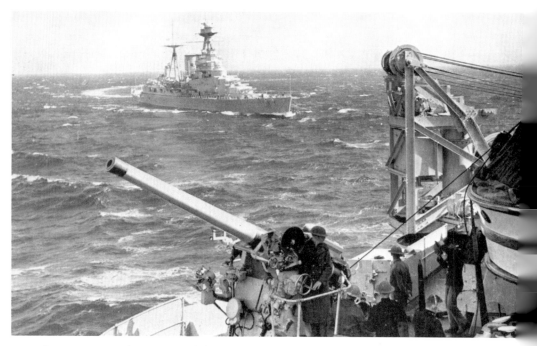

Convoy escorting became one of the major duties of the Royal Navy, and was more and more important as the war ground on. This photograph shows not just the larger escort vessel, but the secondary armament of another escort as well.

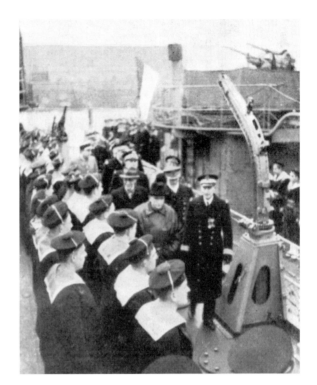

A full inspection of a French torpedo boat is seen taking place. Such inspections were meant to improve morale; in fact, sailors on all sides viewed them as nothing more than a thundering nuisance.

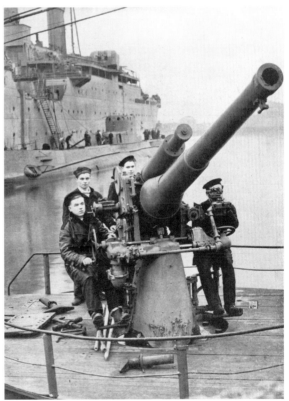

Sailors manning rhe deck gun of a submarine. In the early days of the war, many ships, unescorted and alone, were sunk by gunfire from the U-boats.

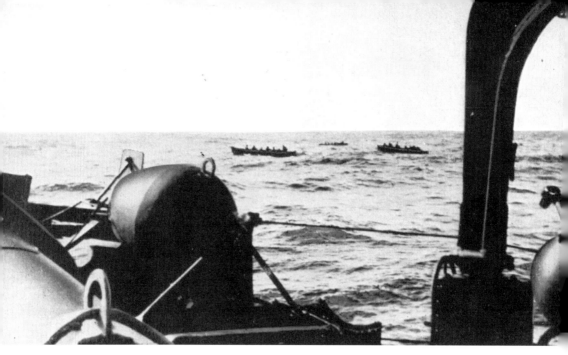

Whalers setting out to rescue the survivors of a sunken U-boat. Rescuing sailors was nearly always attempted once their ship had been sunk. Sadly, such attempts were not always successful.

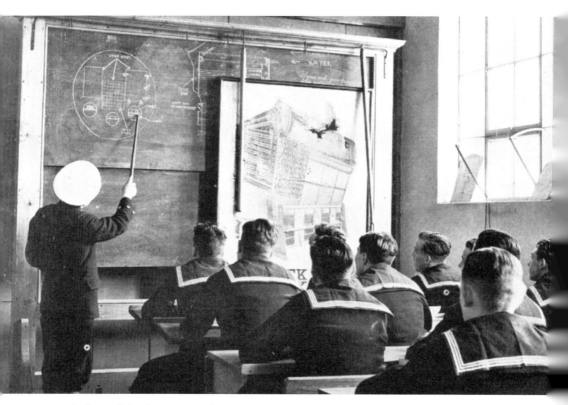

Stoker training for new recruits.